# HAUNTED
# DONEGAL

# HAUNTED
# DONEGAL

## Madeline McCully

*Dedicated to the memory of my parents,*
*James and Kathleen Toland,*
*who nurtured the love of*
*storytelling in their children*

First published 2016

The History Press Ireland
50 City Quay
Dublin 2
Ireland
www.thehistorypress.ie

The History Press Ireland is a member of Publishing Ireland,
the Irish book publishers' association.

British Library Cataloguing in Publication Data.
A catalogue record for this book is available from the British Library.

ISBN 978 1 84588 897 8

Typesetting and origination by The History Press
Printed in Malta, by Melita Press

# CONTENTS

# FOREWORD

GHOST stories! I always find it amazing that in this fast-moving world of ours they still have the power to thrill folk. So, having frequently covered haunted places in broadcasting and writing, I was delighted when Madeline asked me to introduce this follow-up to her book on Derry ghosts.

Madeline and I have exchanged many spooky stories over the years and we worked together for several seasons at the Derry Playhouse on the Winter Ghosts series. During that time, I discovered that Madeline has the true storyteller's art – a wonderfully intimate way of weaving her tales. In this book, she draws us in with clever twists and turns and, to be honest, I sometimes found myself trying to read ahead, so interesting were the yarns.

Another exciting feature of *Haunted Donegal* is the settings. Madeline brings us to such eerie, creepy locations. I was reminded of that chilling movie *Don't Look Now*. You feel you want to turn round and call, 'Is anybody there?' I also enjoyed the wealth of background detail, especially when it related to historical facts and local traditions. This helps to make her stories such a great read and of

course the collection preserves our local folklore for generations to come.

Although I've been in many a haunted room, I've never actually seen a ghost. I did, however, hear something supernatural on a BBC broadcast once and so did those I was with. That's why the crack of the whip in the tale of 'Bess, the Ghost of Gillistown Farmhouse' really made me think there could be something to this business after all.

One story I have personal knowledge of is 'The Spirit of Sharon Rectory'. There is a lot of evidence of this ghost, dating back hundreds of years. I was fortunate enough to be able to visit Sharon and discover for myself how believable the stories about this particular ghost are. I have heard the story of Lord Castlereagh and the apparition of the young child before – it is a very sinister yarn indeed and it is hard to fathom what is at work in the tale. 'Archie's Craw' is another story embedded in Irish tradition. I'm grateful that Madeline's account has a slightly happier ending than some versions I've heard. Last but not least, I must mention 'The Barnesmore Gap Mystery'. This odd story has a flavour of a more modern phenomenon usually known as the hitch-hiker ghost – you know when you're driving along a road late at night and suddenly a stranger appears out of nowhere and flags you down – or, worse still, you suddenly find someone sitting in the back seat – how did they get there? There's some kind of time warp of the kind you see in movies and the Glen Miller aspect of the story is really interesting.

But it is time you experienced these tales for yourself. My advice would be that you curl up on the sofa with Madeline's beautifully crafted book – optional extras might include a roaring log fire and a glass of wine… Now, if you hear a knock or the crack of a whip while you are reading just take a deep breath – ghosts do not bite – or at least that's what I was told. So, there's no need to be afraid … Or is there?

*Ken McCormack, September 2016*

# ACKNOWLEDGEMENTS

A book of ghost stories is not written in isolation, it only comes to fruition with the input from many people. I have been very fortunate over the years in the people I've met that have been willing to share their stories with me.

The first person to mention is Ken McCormack, a collector, broadcaster, writer and a great storyteller in his own right. I thank him for his total availability when I needed help or clarification. Nothing was too much trouble for him and I am extremely grateful. He was encouraging and supportive all the way.

I thank John McLaughlin of Carrowmena for the storytelling evening I spent in his company and that of Andy and Ellen Reed who introduced me to him. Seamus Gallagher, Manager of the Dunlewey Centre is a master storyteller in his own right and I hope I have done justice to his Dunlewey stories. I thank Sean Beattie and Belinda Mehaffey of Donegal Historical Society for their valuable input in The Witch of Loch an Dúin and Nion Ruadh. Joe and Francis Cullen of Rosguill were a delight to listen to when they spoke the Irish language, as was Caoimhin Mac Giolla Bhride who told me the story of Doe Castle.

Thanks to Noeleen Morrison for discovering the story of Gillistown Farmhouse and to Alistair McLaren who clarified the details of this ghost on his family's farm. A very big thank-you to Lisa Tully of Sharon Rectory with whom I spent one of the most interesting afternoons during the writing of this book.

Two contributors who have sadly since died were Bertie Bryce and Michael McGuinness. Bertie was a dear friend and one of the greatest storytellers I have known. He made his stories live in his own inimitable style and I Included the Inch Banshee and the Bridgend Poltergeist as told. Many years ago Michael McGuinness told me the sad story of his grandfather's death in Butte, Montana and the appearance of his wraith in Inishowen.

Ian Cullen of the *Derry Journal* wrote about Father Hegarty's Rock some years ago and I have added some historical background.

I hope that I have done justice to the tales and to the people who told them to me.

A very big thank you to Jim McCallion who gave me much needed help in preparing the photographs for the book. It is difficult to access photographs of times gone by but he was patient and always helpful when I asked for help. To the Donegal Railway Association, Donegal County Council, Donegal Historical Society, Gerry Brady and Seamus Coyle, many thanks for the use of your photographs.

The entire library staff in the Central Library Derry, particularly Maura Craig and Linda Ming who were always on hand to help me in my research. Nothing was too much trouble for them.

Beth Amphlett, Senior Editor of The History Press merits a special mention for her editorial help, so gently given.

I must also thank the Arts Council of Northern Ireland for their awards and support over the years for my story gathering and research.

Lastly, I thank my husband Thomas for his unfailing support, interest and encouragement during the writing and for driving me here there and everywhere in Donegal in pursuit of stories.

# INTRODUCTION

DONEGAL (or '*Dún an nGall*' in Irish, meaning 'the fort of the stranger') is the name given to the most northerly county in Ireland. Strange things have happened, and continue to happen, in this wild and beautiful place and ghost stories are part of the fabric of life here. If stones could only speak, they would have strange and illuminating things to tell us. Perhaps they could tell us how Donegal got its name. Was it from the Vikings who invaded Ireland in the ninth century or the Red Branch Knights of Conor MacNessa who appear in 'The Grianan of Aileach Warriors' story? Or was it from Scottish mercenaries called Gallowglasses ('foreign warriors') who helped Ireland in their battles against the Anglo-Norman invasion in the twelfth century?

In this book, I have included tales of the strangers. The most famous of these were the MacSweeney and O'Donnell clans, which feature in 'The Tragic Lovers of Doe Castle' and 'The Piper's Cave at Fanad'. I hope you will find the stories as interesting to read as they were to research and write.

Storytelling was an essential part of my childhood. During Sunday afternoon walks, my father spun many a tale about the places that we passed, who had lived there, what had happened in that house or farm, what battles had been fought there and many other things. Whether they were true or not wasn't important. His philosophy was 'why let the truth stand in the way of a good story?'

My mother was born in Donegal and our family spent many holidays in my great-aunt's house in Donegal when we were young. There was something eerily seductive about listening to ghost stories around a wide hearth with the glow from a turf fire and the light of a Tilley lamp and then tiptoeing off into the 'lower room' with a candle in a saucer. With the bedclothes pulled up to the chins, our eyes would roam fearfully around the room as we expected a ghost to appear from the gloomy recesses. When the candle finally flickered and died, we whispered our prayers and eventually fell into a dream world akin to the kind of thing you would expect to see in a blockbuster movie.

On other occasions, my mother took us up into the hills or to the nearby beach for a picnic and told us wild and wonderful stories of the 'olden days' in the

countryside. Mamore Gap was a favourite walk and we made the journey up to the holy well there so often that I believe I know every stone along the way. It is for this reason that I included 'The Mamore Gap's Ghostly Travellers'.

I miss those days and I was often reminded of how special they were when I interviewed people about their experiences, particularly in the remoter areas of the county.

I am sad that the oral tradition of storytelling is gradually disappearing as technology allows for more and more electronic communication. This book is an attempt to preserve some of the stories told in and about Donegal. Many are documented already and it has been a joy to research them. Others come 'straight from the mouth'.

I hope that you enjoy reading them as much as I have enjoyed gathering them.

# 1

# CASTLES
# AND MANORS

### Castlereagh and the Goblin Child

The following tale was recorded by Sir Walter Scott's biographer, John Gibson Lockhart. Scott himself had heard the tale from Lord Castlereagh who had told the story at one of his wife's dinner parties in Paris in 1815.

Lord Castlereagh.

In 1793, Robert Stewart, son of Lord Castlereagh, was a young captain and a member of the Dublin parliament, was posted to the old and somewhat dilapidated barracks in Ballyshannon, where he commanded a militia regiment.

He did not allow his military duties to interfere with his great love of hunting. On one occasion, during the gaming season in November, he pursued game much farther than he had intended and lost his way. When the weather took a turn for the worse he put the idea of shooting pheasants out of his mind and looked for a place to ride out the storm.

He presented himself at the door of a gentleman's house, sent in his card and requested shelter for the night. The hospitality of the Irish country gentry is proverbial; the master of the house received him warmly, explained that he could not make him so comfortable as he could have wished because his house was full of visitors already. In addition to his visitors, some strangers, fleeing the inclemency of the night, had already come to the door, seeking shelter.

The master called the butler and bade him do the best he could under the circumstances to provide a room for the captain. The room to which he was shown was very large. It did not contain much furniture and seemed cold and draughty. Captain Stewart requested that a fire of wood and turf be lit in the gaping, old-fashioned hearth in a vain attempt to heat the room. What happened next was an experience that haunted Robert Stewart.

'I woke up in the middle of the night for some unaccountable reason. The fire at the far end of the room was but a gentle glow and as I lay watching the dying embers it suddenly blazed up.'

The brightest light emanated from the chimney itself and startled Stewart, but what happened next startled him even more.

'From the embers stepped the glowing, radiant naked figure of a small boy and he walked towards me. I could not believe my eyes and wondered if I was dreaming but I pinched myself and knew that I was not.'

Initially, the young captain was paralysed with fear, and as the figure walked slowly towards him, it grew in stature at every step until, in the words of Scott's biographer John Gibson Lockhart, 'on coming within two or three paces of his bed, it had assumed the appearance of a ghastly giant, pale as death, with a bleeding wound on the brow, and eyes glaring with rage and despair'.

Captain Stewart jumped out of bed and faced the figure in an attitude of defiance, at which point it drew back, diminishing in size until eventually the childlike form vanished back into the embers.

The following morning, Stewart voiced his anger at the breakfast table, believing that the master or his guests had played some sort of prank, but they all denied this accusation.

Suddenly a thought seemed to strike the master. He called his butler.

'Hamilton', he said, 'where did Captain Stewart sleep last night?'

'Well, sir, you know that every room was filled last night so I gave him the boy's room. But I was sure that the fire would keep *him* from coming out.'

His host admonished the butler and took the captain aside to clarify what he had seen. He explained that there was a tradition in his family that 'whomever the Radiant Boy appeared to would rise to the summit of power but when he reached that he would die a violent death'.

When his father died, Robert Stewart inherited the title of Lord Castlereagh and he later became a senior government minister. He helped to defeat Napoleon and was key in the Congress of Vienna that led to peace in Europe for decades. He was blamed, however, for the Peterloo Massacre, when cavalry with drawn sabres charged a crowd who were demonstrating in Manchester for universal suffrage.

It was because of this massacre that the poet Shelley wrote, in his poem 'The Masque of Anarchy', 'I met Murder on the way. He had a face like Castlereagh.'

Perhaps it was this scandal that led him to take his own life, but many, including Scott, believed that 'The Goblin Child' continued to haunt him and drove him to take that final violent step, of taking his own life, as prophesied.

The story inspired William Allingham, a poet who was born in the town of Ballyshannon, to write a poem called the 'Goblin Child of Ballyshannon':

This happened when our island still
Had nests of goblins left to fill,

Each mouldy nook and corner close
Like soldiers in an ancient house.
And this one read within the face
Intruding on its dwelling place
Lines of woe, despair and blood.
By spirits only understood;
As mortals now can read the same
In the letters to his name.
Who in that haunted chamber lay,
When we call him Castlereagh.

## Mongevlin Castle

The most famous haunting of Mongevlin Castle is that the Ingean Dubh spectre, a dark-haired faceless woman garbed in white who prowls the castle and its grounds. But she is not the only ghost who resides in that dreary place. The castle's history might shed some light on the identities of these spectres.

'Mongevlin Castle is situated about one mile from the village of St. Johnston and seven miles from Derry.' So wrote Captain Pynnar in 1619 when he mentioned its location in his 'Survey of the Escheated Counties of Ulster'. He also reported that 'Sir John Stewart hath three thousand acres, called Cashell, Hetin and Littergull. Upon this proportion there is built at *Magelvin* a very strong Castle with a flanker at each corner.'

The walls of the courtyard and gateway, erected between the River Foyle and the castle, were standing until a few years ago, according to the *Dublin Penny Journal*, published in the 1830s. A small stone flag with the following inscription of John Stewart's ownership was built into the arch:

J.S
E.S.T
1619

This stone was lost but another one remains which might give some clue about the ghosts that haunted the castle. The inscription bore the words, 'The Hon. Elizabeth Hamilton, daughter of John, Lord Culpepper and widow of Colonel James Hamilton (who lost his life at sea in Spain in the service of King and Country) purchased this manor and annexed it to the opposite estate of the family.' The inscription went on the say that Elizabeth was very generous to her numerous offspring, settling them with money and estates. Her eldest son James, Earl of Abercorn and Viscount Strabane 'caused this inscription to be placed here for the information of her posterity. Anno 1704.'

James II stopped at the castle for a short time during the Siege of Derry and from there sent proposals of surrender to the garrison through his host, Archdeacon Hamilton.

There was a young servant lad who worked in the castle in the eighteenth century. One winter night he visited a neighbouring farmhouse and confessed to his friend that he was frightened. He told him that some nights he saw strange forms rushing to and fro, especially in the upper rooms. James, for that was the young boy's name, stammered out stories of fearful yelling and screaming. He told of what he had heard in the kitchen from the other servants about the frightening goings-on when the hour of midnight approached. He received no comfort from his friend, who said that the castle was indeed haunted but reminded him that he was lucky to be able to work there to help his family.

The lad walked back to the castle alone. As he approached the grounds, he heard a clock in the church tower strike midnight. Immediately he was overcome with a weak and shivery feeling, as if some malevolent thing was watching him. He tried to run but the weakness made his legs buckle beneath him and as he fell to the ground he heard a fearful screech. He fainted and the terrifying noise was lost in a silent blackness.

When he came to, he rose unsteadily and, as soon as he was able to, he took to his heels and ran, but no matter how fast he moved he still heard the rustle of something or someone right behind him. When he reached the servants' door it was locked and he was unable to open it. James shouted and banged on the heavy wood with his fists but no one came. He turned around, fearful of what he might see and there it was – a glowing, luminescent being dressed in a loose white cape with a hood. To his horror, he saw that it had no face. Was this the Ingean Dubh spectre? As it moved towards him, he cowered in the doorway. At that moment, the housekeeper opened the door and the young boy fell in.

'What ails ye?' she cried. 'You are as white as a ghost.'

With that, she hauled him inside. He couldn't speak and just pointed to the open door. The housekeeper looked out but the spectre had disappeared. She brought the lad into the kitchen and gave him a bowl of hot milk and sent him off to bed.

For the next two days all was quiet, but on the third night the boy went to bed but could not rest. In every moan that the wind made as it blew through the old and broken roof of the castle, he heard the wailings and screams of unearthly beings.

The following morning, he went home to his relations and told them that he could no longer stay in that place. They didn't believe him and thought that he was making an excuse to leave his employment. They were in need of the money he earned, so they insisted that he return. He did so, but he continued to be tortured by the ghostly apparitions and noises that played havoc with his young mind. One morning, 'he was found suspended by the neck, a stiffened corpse!'

It is said that his spirit joined the other spirits in their ghostly midnight vigil at Mongevlin Castle.

## The Blue Lady of Ards

In the dark shadow of Muckish Mountain in County Donegal, there are many strange tales told of ghostly encounters with banshees, eerie figures, black cats and headless coachmen. There are also tales of manifestations of women, one of which is known as the Blue Lady of Ards.

The Wray family from Yorkshire built a magnificent house in Donegal in the year 1708. The house stood on a promontory jutting out into Sheephaven Bay. The family chose the location for the spectacular panorama it offered and the house was designed to take full advantage of the view. It was considered to be one of the most beautiful residences in the whole of the county of Donegal.

In 1780, the Wray family sold the house and lands to the Stewart family of Ards, County Down, although it is said that the Stewarts were then given all of the lands around Creeslough for services to the Crown of England. They named their estate Ards after their County Down roots on the Ards Peninsula. Such was the fame of their mansion that among the landlords and the social elite of Donegal, invitations to the Stewart home were much sought after.

*Ards House.*

The Stewarts, later known as the Stewart Bams, did not have any social interaction with the local people. One of the ladies of the manor apparently objected to seeing the estate workers toiling on the Sabbath so she persuaded her husband to have a 40-foot tunnel built from the estate to St John's Church of Ireland church. In this way, she was able to attend church without having to look at the lowly workers.

However, like many of the owners of the big houses in Ireland the Stewarts could not afford its upkeep and it was sold to the Capuchin Order in 1930, when its name was changed to Ard Mhuire. In January 1931, it became the Novitiate and Theological Seminary of the Order.

It would seem that the ghost of the Blue Lady did not appear until then – at least, there was no talk among the gentry or the servants of such an apparition. Perhaps the presence of priests had something to do with it. No one really knows, but one must ask if the Blue Lady's secret lies with the Stewart family. The apparition was seen hovering at the top of the magnificent horseshoe staircase, where the two flights of stairs running up each side from the hall met on the landing. The bannisters were carved out of rich oak and in the heyday of the Stewart family, these stairs rang with the footsteps of ladies and their maids.

Did the lady in blue wait on the landing for her husband's return? Or did she observe some dreadful happening below in the hall? We will never know. Could she have been the lady who despised the lowly peasants? Was this her punishment – that her restless spirit should have to haunt the house?

All we know is that her ghost has been seen several times. Once a priest felt a strange presence above him when he was walking upstairs. When he raised his eyes, he was astonished to see a beautiful lady dressed in a blue gown standing motionless at the top of the stairs. He felt no fear, but crossed to the other flight of stairs to avoid her. Although he swore that he did not see her move, she was standing at the top of the second flight too. He paused, but then continued to climb. At the top, he avoided looking at the lady and passed her without incident.

The priests had no fear of the apparition whose unearthly form they frequently saw on the upper floor, passing them in the passageway or floating from room to room. However, for the sake of the new novices who resided there, the friars undertook to 'house' the lady in one room.

Whatever service or ceremony they performed, the spectre of the Blue Lady did not appear again. It was known, however, that the door of one room was locked and its windows were sealed. It is thought that the spirit of the Lady in Blue had finally been calmed.

Still, curiosity is hard to stifle and often visitors to the friary stood gazing up at the blocked windows and addressed questions about the Blue Lady to the monks. It is interesting that none of them ever directly answered these questions or divulged any information about the ghostly apparition. The visitors were left wondering about the mysterious presence of the Blue Lady in such a beautiful and peaceful place.

A new friary and chapel replaced the old mansion of the Stewart family in 1966, but although the ghost has not appeared to anyone since, the mystery still haunts the minds of those who visit.

## The Tragic Lovers of Doe Castle

Wild are thy hills, O Donegal, that
    frown and darkly rise
As if to greet the mist that falls upon
    them from the skies.
Dark, dark thy hills, and darker still thy
    mountain torrents flow
But none so dark as Maolmuire's heart,
    in his castle hall at Doe.

Few castles are without their ghostly legends. Doe Castle is no exception. Built in 1425 on a rocky promontory that juts out onto an inlet of Sheephaven Bay, the water guards its northern, eastern and southern sides. A drawbridge over a deep moat protects the approach by land on its western side and a portcullis spans the archway into the courtyard. Storms race across the wild hills of Donegal, which look menacingly down on the castle, and brackish torrents of water flow roughly into the bay.

On stormy nights, or when the mist hugs the mountaintops, it is easy to imagine that the castle holds dark secrets – secrets as dark as the heart of the chieftain Maolmhuire MacSweeney, who lived within the walls of Doe Castle in 1620.

Strange as it may be, the proud and wealthy but black-hearted Maolmhuire had a sweet daughter, Aileen, whose beauty was celebrated by poets. So fair was her hair that it was compared to moonbeams and her smile was 'like the opening of a flower'. Such a lovely young woman was destined to love and be loved and so it happened that Turlough Óg O'Boyle saw Aileen MacSweeney one day when out hunting deer and hare in Dunally Wood. On his very first meeting, he fell deeply in love with her and she with him.

*Doe Castle.*

Turlough was no ordinary young man. Apart from being strong and handsome, he was the chieftain of the O'Boyle clan, one of the most important clans of Donegal. He was described as being 'the pride of Faugher side and as strong as the oak, as straight as the ash and as swift on his feet as the deer'. From Gweedore to Fanad, none could equal his feats of strength. In rain, hail, frost or snow, he led his huntsmen on their expeditions and on many a Christmas Day he was known to hunt the wild deer of Glenveagh. He feared no man or beast and stories of his exploits spread to the far reaches of Donegal.

He often met his Aileen secretly in Dunally Wood on the pretext of hunting deer. It was well known in the area that Aileen's father guarded his daughter jealously. His plans to marry her to a chieftain of his choosing took no account of her wishes. When he noticed that she was more vivacious than usual, he became suspicious, especially of her

frequent absences. He decided to follow her on one of her expeditions and was outraged when he saw her fly into the arms of Turlough. Unbeknownst to the two of them, he watched the passionate embrace of the young lovers and his rage knew no bounds. In the heat of his anger, he confronted them and swore that Turlough Óg would never marry his daughter. He forcefully dragged her away, forbidding her to look back.

When the young man heard her scream his name he was distraught. In an attempt to see her again, he took a boat to the Lackagh stream that flowed by Doe Castle. He disguised himself as a poor fisherman and pretended to fish, casting a line out again and again. Aileen, imprisoned high in the castle, was unaware of his presence, but this was not true of her father. Convinced that the young man would try to see Aileen, he posted lookouts among the trees that bordered the river and lake. After some days, they reported to Maolmhuire that his suspicions about the fisherman were well founded. MacSweeney had two boats, each manned by two men, launched and ready to waylay Turlough as he passed Bishop's Isle, a small, uninhabited crannog in the lake. Although taken by surprise, Turlough put up a manly fight, but he was eventually overpowered and taken prisoner by the four men as Aileen's father looked on. On Maolmhuire's orders, he was thrown into the dungeon of the castle and put in chains.

Aileen, confined to a bleak room high in the tower, was unaware that for three days her young lover was below. On the fourth day, she heard the tramping of feet across the drawbridge. Filled with curiosity, she went to the top battlements to look down. She beheld four stalwart men bearing a bier wrapped in a funeral pall. She watched as the bier was carried to the castle graveyard and roughly placed on the ground. The men dug a deep hole and rested for a while, sitting on the mound of clay and making raucous remarks about the corpse beside them. With a slowly dawning horror, she waited and when the pall was removed her fears were confirmed. Young Turlough's body, pale and still in death, rested on the bier.

Then with a terrible shriek she madly
    leapt from the tower to the ground
Where by her faithful waiting maid her
    corpse it cold was found.
And in Doe Castle graveyard green
    beneath the mouldering soil
Maolmuire's daughter sleeps in death
    with Turlough Óg O'Boyle

Sweet Aileen met her lover in one last embrace before she died. Maolmhuire was inconsolable. It is said that he bitterly regretted his actions and that he knew not a moment of peace from that time until his own death. In his despair, he allowed his daughter to be laid to rest beside her beloved Turlough.

They sleep together in death, as they never could in life, in Castleween Cemetery near the castle. There is a legend that a rose bush grew atop each grave and the branches entwined and produced the most beautiful and fragrant of blossoms.

Some visitors to the castle say that they have seen an apparition of a young woman dressed in a dark cloak, standing still and looking over the battlements. Perhaps they have and perhaps the story of a boat slowly gliding over Sheephaven with two figures in it, their arms entwined, while a soft breeze whispers music, is also true.

Tradition holds that the ghosts of Turlough Óg O'Boyle and Aileen haunt

*MacSweeney's tombstone.*

the lake and the castle and, although they have been seen many times, it is said that in death they finally found the peace they could not find in life.

> And fishers say that along the beach a
> phantom boat is seen
> To gently glide by pale moonlight
> a-down by Lackagh stream
> While in that boat two figures float and
> on each face a smile
> They say it is young Aileen and her
> Turlough Óg O'Boyle.

(From the poem by Niall Mac Giolla Bhríde)

## The Ghostly Swans and Burt Castle

Burt Castle was built around 1560–1580 and was originally on an island surrounded by marshland. It was just one of many castles built by the O'Doherty clan, who were known as the 'Lords of Inishowen'. Sean Mór O'Dochartaigh became Sir John O'Doherty when Henry VIII knighted him in 1541, the year Henry became King of Ireland.

Sir Cahir O'Doherty, his son, took up residence in Burt in 1601 upon the death of his father Sir John. It is believed that it was during his time at the castle that one of his kinsmen seduced a young girl from the neighbouring area with promises of marriage, money and position. When she became pregnant, the man refused to marry her. Not only did he refuse. He also claimed that she was the one who had seduced him. He spread the rumour amongst the other soldiers and soon their salacious remarks reached the ears of her father. Such was his rage that he ordered his daughter to leave and never to return. The girl rushed from her home and that night she walked to the water's edge and paced along the shore of Lough Swilly, wailing and weeping about her misfortune.

*Swans at Burt.*

While the full moon shone and glinted on the waters of the lough, two swans swam towards her as if they heard and understood her sadness. They called to her in a particularly plaintive way to offer comfort. When they swam away she stood alone for several moments, then waded into the cold waters of Loch Swilly and drowned.

Her father regretted his harsh reaction and went in search of his daughter, but alas all he found was her body lying among the reeds, with two swans swimming silently nearby. He was distraught. He blamed himself and the man who had brought her to this. At that moment, he vowed that he would avenge his daughter's death.

His daughter was laid to rest and that same night, armed with a long knife, her father went to the castle. It was a formidable fortress, three storeys high, with two circular watchtowers, but he tricked the soldier on duty, pretending that he knew his daughter's lover. Once he found out where the soldier was, he crept up the turnpike staircase in the south-west tower. The man who had betrayed his daughter lay asleep in the vaulted mural chamber on the first floor. The girl's father stabbed him with his long knife and pushed his body through an opening. It fell to the ground with a thud loud enough to alert the sentry.

Feet pounded up the staircase and soldiers rushed into the chamber with swords drawn. Her father did not attempt to protect himself but cursed the O'Doherty kinsman responsible.

'May the O'Doherty feel the pain of loss,' he cried out as the soldiers charged towards him. He died bravely, knowing that he had avenged his daughter.

Was it some kind of poetic justice or was it due to the curse that Sir Cahir's wife, Mary Preston, was kidnapped from the castle? She was the daughter of Viscount Gormanstown, the senior viscount of Ireland, and was kept under arrest in Dublin while her husband was embroiled in a rebellion against England. Sir Cahir lamented her capture and swore to have her back but within a few short weeks, on 5 July 1608, the O'Doherty was killed near Kilmacrennan and the castle eventually fell into the hands of Sir Arthur Chichester, who had quelled the rebellion. The O'Doherty's wife lived to hear that her husband's head was displayed atop a pike outside Newgate Prison like that of a common felon, but she was given and accepted a pension of £40 per annum. Perhaps there was little love lost in that relationship.

The spirit of the girl who died for love lingered on the shores of Lough Swilly. When the moon is full, the swans congregate at the point closest to Burt Castle and let out a cacophony of wailing. It is said that the ghostly figure of the young girl can be seen drifting into the water until she gradually fades beneath the waves.

One farmer who went out there during a snowstorm to find some lost sheep swore that the cries of the swans led him to save his flock and when he freed the last sheep from the snow a beautiful young girl appeared before him and gradually retreated into the waters of the lough.

At the base of the castle walls, there is a certain patch of grass that withers when the swans weep. Is this the spot where the body of the man who wronged the innocent girl fell? Or is it 'hungry grass', where starved Famine victims dropped and died as they foraged for food?

## The Green Lady of Dunlewy

This is a story told to me by Seamus Gallagher, the manager of Ionad Cois Locha at Dunlewey, about that lonely house across the lake. The tale may explain the ghostly appearance of a woman, known as the Green Lady.

'A man called Dumbray was the first landlord and he was not a compassionate man by any means. He evicted the Sweeney family from the estate and the old lady, Mrs Sweeney herself, said to the landlord, "*Ba cuid leat agat a ní páistí ar son*", which translated means "You'll have company but no children".

'And that curse, if one might call it that, seems to have been borne out for there were no children ever born and reared there on that estate. Any family that came there never had a child to follow them. It is said that that's why so many

*The Green Lady of Dunlewey House.*

landlords moved away: to escape the curse. The children that they already had came with them but no more children ever followed their arrival in the house. It is obvious that they believed that part of the curse.

'If you have a mind to go over to the graveyard at Gortahork there, on the right-hand side you can see the headstone that says, "Sweeney, evicted from Dunlewy". It's plain to be seen.

'To this very day, it is well known that anybody who saw this ghost will never go back to that estate. The people that live up there would tell you of the noises in the house, they would. It was unreal, especially at certain times of the night.

When we were young we went up to steal the apples from the orchard where there was a plum tree at the end of the house. There were three of us, the oldest being John Sharkey – he died – and his brother Philip, who's living in Glasgow now, and myself. Now, the first fella went up the tree and took some plums and put them into his pocket. He was level with the second-floor window at this stage and whatever he saw he just jumped right off the tree and never said anything. The second fella went up, took one look at the window and he jumped off the tree too. I was the third going up and I took a couple of plums and I looked at the window and I had to look again to see if my eyes were playing tricks. What I saw scared the living daylights out of me for there was this greenish-greyish figure and I knew that this was the one that I'd heard about. She was an old, old woman with grey straggly hair under a shawl and an expression I couldn't describe. Her eyes were staring straight at me and I looked away for fear that she would reach out for me.

'There was no way to go down that tree easy. I just jumped and the three of us took to our heels and ran. But being boys, and not wanting to seem scared of a figure in a window, the three of us got our courage gathered up and we went back up the tree again. Sure, we convinced ourselves that it might just be a shadow or the moon or something.

'You couldn't see it until you got up to the level of the window and we looked at her again and what happened then scared the living daylights out of us again for didn't she rise and get closer to the window and open her mouth as if she was cursing us or something.

'"This is enough," we said and we jumped down and away we went and never looked back at that window for didn't we have fear that her eyes might be following us. All I can tell you is this: none of us ever wanted to go up there again. I know that I'll never go next or near that place again and that's the truth.'

# 2

# GHOSTLY WARNINGS

## Bess, the Ghost of Gillistown Farmhouse

The Gillistown farmhouse near Drumenan now lies derelict and partly demolished but the haunted living room and passage were still there to be seen in 2004. Few people have approached it since then for fear that they might be 'visited' by the ghost that was said to herald death and serious illness.

James McCausland, the unmarried owner of Gillistown, lived in the farmhouse with his widowed sister Sarah. In 1928, after a heavy fall, James' health deteriorated and he was taken down to his brother William's home nearby, in Drumenan. This left Sarah alone in Gillistown. At the time, Sarah was beginning to show signs of dementia. Margaret McCausland was just an 11-year-old schoolgirl when her mother, fearing for Sarah, who was prone to wander during the hours of darkness, sent Margaret to stay with her at night.

This was a big responsibility for a young girl. With a certain amount of reluctance, she did what her mother wished. After attending school in St Johnston, she went to her own home in Drumenan. Once she had finished her evening meal, Margaret picked up her schoolbag and left at six o'clock to walk the quarter-mile to Gillistown. There the young girl would sit at the kitchen table with her Aunt Sarah and her pet dog Spot. While trying to do her homework, Margaret was often disturbed by her aunt's singing and the dog howling a descant. Margaret recalled in later years that it was 'like living in a madhouse'!

Margaret slept with Sarah in an upstairs room and soon got used to the creaks and groans of the old house as the temperature fell at night. One night, however, she was suddenly awoken by a noise like that of a whip or a thin stick being struck across the table downstairs in the living room. Frightened by the unexpected noise, she woke her aunt. They both heard another three or four loud strokes on the table below very clearly. Margaret was terrified but her aunt simply took her hand and told her not to be frightened because it was only 'Bess' warning the McCauslands that sometime soon a member of the family was either going to die or suffer a serious illness.

Margaret hardly slept. Charlie Donald, a neighbour, arrived at 6 a.m. to feed the horses just as Margaret was about to leave for Drumenan. She asked if he had heard of the ghost. Charlie confirmed that he knew of Bess, but he assured Margaret that the ghost was friendly and would not harm anyone.

The following night, she once again found herself suddenly wide awake. This time she heard the sound of heavy footsteps walking up and down the corridor that linked the living room and the kitchen right below her bedroom. Again Aunt Sarah tried to calm her niece, telling her that the footsteps would soon stop. Margaret realised that if she was to tell her mother she would receive no sympathy or understanding from her.

The hauntings became more sinister when Bess's warnings became a reality.

On 19 July 1928, James McCausland died in Drumenan. This was only a short time after the ghostly warnings were heard in Gillistown farmhouse. James never returned to Gillistown after his fall. Margaret continued to stay overnight with her aunt at Gillistown until she was badly scalded on the legs by boiling water in the farm kitchen. By this time, Sarah's dementia had worsened and she was brought down to Drumenan to be cared for until she died.

Only later did Margaret discover that her elder sister Isobel had earlier refused to sleep in the Gillistown house when asked to do so by her mother. She too had heard of the ghost.

Margaret also remembered that she had been forbidden to enter the 'haunted' living room. It always remained locked and the only person who was allowed to go in was the minister when he came to visit.

*In August 2004, Alistair McLaren, a nephew of Margaret, and his wife Sadie visited the ruined Gillistown farmhouse with another cousin. They photographed the previously haunted passageway and living room. It would seem that the ghost also left when the last person to live there died.*

The haunted farmhouse at Gillistown.

# The Blue Stack's Banshee

The Blue Stack Mountains are in a wild and lonely but beautiful part of Donegal. A youth leader named Marie O'Donnell (not her real name) once accompanied a group of young people on an out-door pursuit project to the Blue Stack Mountains. Since there were three youth leaders, each worker had some free time allocated to them. When her group were off on a trip, Marie, who was a keen photographer, decided to take advantage of her free time. The evening tempera-ture had cooled but since there was still ample daylight she decided to explore one of the walks in preparation for an excursion with her group the following day. She put her camera and tripod into her rucksack and set off.

She didn't intend to go very far but the mysterious and beautiful landscape beckoned and so she lost track of time. Entranced by the view, she slipped off her rucksack and stood on the track drinking in the solitude and peacefulness of the mountainside. Without warning, the wind began to rise and dusky clouds swirled across the hilltops. She looked at her watch and turned quickly, knowing that she would need to hurry if she were to get back to the centre before dark.

The rain spattered against her face and wind gusted around her angrily. The bright sky of the early evening had turned a sullen, seething grey and strange cloud patterns were forming. A strong feeling of uneasiness filled her. She tried to quicken her pace, but the wind whipped and snapped around her, forcing her backwards. She bent over almost double to try to push into the wind, hoping to make headway, but for each step forward she stumbled two steps backwards. She dug her walking poles into the earth, which was now boggy. She realised that she had strayed off the track and stopped to get her bearings.

*The Blue Stack's Banshee.*

Her eyes watered because of the ferocity of the wind and she shivered, thinking that she would never reach the safety of the centre.

What happened next made her shudder. 'And to this day,' she said recently, 'I nearly suffocated with the fear and panic that gripped me. A dark cloud swirled around me, whipping up the ferns and heather to frenzy. The ground seemed to move beneath my feet and the sound of the wind became a shriek, so loud and piercing that I couldn't hear anything else.' She swung round and round, holding her hands over her ears to try to escape the screech.

The wind stopped suddenly and fell silent, but that was not the end of her encounter. What came next was more horrible than what had gone before. The air was filled with a horrible stench, so putrid that she vomited and fell to her knees on the path. As she tried to rise, the wind rose again and she was confronted with a strange figure with wild eyes and straggling hair that blew towards her and wound itself around her throat. The figure pulled her to the ground and a sound like a scratchy whisper began saying something over and over again. She later compared the sensation to 'insects crawling into her ears'.

Again the wind fell and she rose to her feet with the help of her walking poles. The sullen clouds had disappeared and although it was dusk by then the air was clear. There was nothing around her to explain the experience that she had just had.

She made a quick sign of the cross and took to her heels, running as fast as she could. When she saw the lights of the centre she slowed down, reluctant to let the young people see the state she was in. Only when she composed herself did she enter and make the effort to greet the other group leaders.

At dinner that night someone passed her a note from the office. It read, 'A message came for you but whoever it was said that they will phone in the morning.'

Next morning, she received word that an uncle had died. When she thought of the whispered words that she had heard on her walk the previous evening it dawned on her that it was his name that had been whispered to her.

Some time later, her father spoke of the banshee's visit to him before his brother died and when Maria related her experience to him he just nodded and said, 'That's her alright. We seem to be one of the families she visits and sure it's not a pleasant thing to happen.'

Maria confessed that she lives in dread of the next visit and prays that there will not be one.

## Father Hegarty's Rock

One might wonder what the Penal days in Ireland and the spectral appearance of a rearing white horse have in common. The answer lies in the legend that surrounds the murder of a holy friar just outside Buncrana on the Inishowen Peninsula, County Donegal

Although the British did not introduce the Penal Laws in Ireland until 1698, there were many attempts to stamp out the 'priest-ridden subservience' of the people in the remote northern promontory of Donegal.

Two royal proclamations preceded the Penal Laws in 1604 and 1611. These forbade the celebration of Mass and declared that all priests should be banished from the country. Many priests ignored this despicable law and continued to travel around the countryside, saying Mass in houses, caves and even high in the hills.

In 1632, one holy man, Friar Hegarty of Buncrana, continued to serve his flock. He travelled the length of the west coast of Lough Swilly, from Fahan to Desertegney and even beyond, over Mamore Gap to Urris. Although his actions were 'unlawful' in the eyes of the British, he was able to pass safely from one place to another with the help of people hungry for the word of God. At times he lived in caves or outhouses and sometimes in secret rooms within homesteads but his main abode was in Lisnakelly in a cave sheltered by trees and gorse near Porthaw Glen.

His congregation was sworn to secrecy for it was well known that if he were discovered, those disregarding the law by harbouring him would be either executed or deported. Only his sister, who lived nearby, had access to his hiding place. He could not light a fire for heat for fear that it would give away his hiding place, so his sister, a godly woman, made the hiding place as comfortable as possible with straw and home-woven woollen blankets for his bed. Late at night or before dawn, she brought food to him and in that way he had the strength to preach and say Mass.

One night his sister's husband, curious about her 'nocturnal wanderings', decided to follow her. When she pushed aside the bushes and entered the cave, he crept closer and recognised the voice of his brother-in-law, Friar Hegarty. He crept silently away and was in bed when she returned, pretending to be asleep.

The following day, on the pretext that he was going to Buncrana to buy seed, he reported the good friar to the English authorities. He received 'Judas money' in return for his treachery. Someone from the friar's congregation saw him colluding with the Redcoat officer and hurried to warn the priest.

A neighbouring farmer gave the priest his prize white horse and he galloped away just as the Redcoats were approaching. The horse flew over the gorse and the rocks towards Stragill, where a boat was supposed to be waiting to ferry him to Fanad. The horse leapt to the rocks but alas there was no boat waiting for him. The priest jumped off his horse, dove into the water and began to swim towards Rathmullan. Unfortunately, the tide was coming in and he made little headway. The soldiers shouted to him to return and offered him a pardon. Exhausted from trying to fight the current, he saw some of the Redcoats standing on the rocks, reaching out as if to offer him assistance. He swam towards the shore. The soldiers pulled him out and forced him to the ground and on the captain's command he was beheaded with a sword.

Legend has it that the good friar's head bounced on the grass of the mossy cliff edge nine times and that grass has never grown in these nine places since. The bare patches defy explanation and can still be seen today. The promontory on which he met his death cracked, leaving a distinctive cross shape, which is said to have been formed at the moment of the Friar Hegarty's death.

It is also thought that the white horse given to help Father Hegarty escape perished when it leapt over a precipice onto the rocks below. There is what appears to be an imprint of a horseshoe cut into the rock in this place.

In January 2003, Ian Cullen, writing for the *Derry Journal*, told the story of the appearance of the white steed near the point where the horse is supposed to have disappeared.

Four young boys from the Buncrana area took advantage of the newly tarmacked path leading from Buncrana Castle to Father Hegarty's Rock. They were astride their quad bikes, showing off to each other.

The boys' escapade was a dangerous one as the light was fading and it was growing dark. The leading biker looked behind him, shouting to his friends just as they approached a particularly dangerous part of the path. At that point, there is a sheer drop of several feet and little to stop anyone plunging onto the rocks below. When he turned around again, he braked hard, terrified at the spectre of a white horse before him.

The huge white steed appeared out of nowhere and stood on its hind legs, towering over the horrified boy. The sheen of the horse appeared to light up the sky around him and when he looked he saw the waves crashing against the rocks far below. The other boys realised that they had been only seconds from their death when they were stopped by the horse. As they watched, the horse took a flying leap off the precipice and vanished.

The boys were unable to move, both frightened and relieved at the same time. After a few moments, they turned back without saying a word. It was only when they reached the old fort at Ned's Point that they looked at each other and spoke of what they had seen and experienced. There was no doubt in their minds that the appearance of the horse had saved them from serious injury and possibly even death.

*Fr Hegarty's phantom horse.*

Even afterwards they were reluctant to talk about that night. Since then very few people venture there once darkness settles in. All one can hear is the sound of the waves on the rocks when blackness envelops the coast.

Another appearance of a floating figure was reported by a young couple who sat down near the spot where Fr Hegarty met his gruesome death, but they 'felt no fear, only a heavy sadness' emanating from the figure.

The spooky setting and the grim history of Fr Hegarty keeps the legend alive.

## The Wraiths at Dunlewy Bridge

Seamus Gallagher, the manager of Ionad Cois Locha at Dunlewey, had this story to tell.

'We had a function here about thirty odd years ago. It was a fundraising one and we held it up in the community centre and I must admit that we served drink at it. But the drinking wasn't all our doing for some of the people who came from other places that night also had their drink with them. It was a grand night and when it was over it was about half past two in the morning.

'I went down with my dancing partner to leave her home and drove back up the road. On the way back I came across an accident. A car had hit the bridge head-on and one of the four people in the car was one that I knew from the dance.

'It was a terrible tragedy that one of them was killed.

'What a mess. There was blood every-where and for a long while we tried to open the car doors to get them all out,

*Wraiths at Dunlewy Bridge.*

but we couldn't manage it. There was nothing for it but to break the back windows and only then were we able to pull them out. We tried to do some first aid on them because we'd learnt that from our mountain rescue work. Living so close to Errigal, we had a goodly amount of practise rescuing people from the mountain who needed medical help.

'Well I don't know what prompted me to say it but I did say that night, "Two people are going to die from this accident." One of them was serious but unconscious and he only lived for ten days after that. There was a priest there that night and I said to him and other people heard me say again, "Two people are going to die here."

'The priest said to me, "How do you make that out?"

'All I can say is this. I had a premonition some years earlier – I don't know exactly how many years ago it was, but I was coming up that road from a dance and it was four or five in the morning. Now there were very few cars on that wee road all those years ago.

'I saw two fellas crossing the road in front of me down at the bridge, just dressed in their working clothes, but they disappeared and I thought they were hiding on me so I stopped the car. I shone the lights across the road and got out of the car. I went over to the bridge, which was a wee one, built around 1840, and it not the height of a table. I looked over it and one minute I saw them standing there and the next minute there was no one at all. It would have been impossible to get under it but there was not a sign of the fellas at all.

'I asked myself often that night afterwards, "Where did these people go?" I had searched around but there was

nothing. I can tell you that I had the strangest feeling that there was something not quite right about what I'd seen.

'When that accident happened on the night of the fundraising, I was one of the first people to arrive at it and that thing that had happened all those years ago was on my mind. It came right back to me that that was a premonition that I'd had all those years ago when the two wraiths of those fellas disappeared right at that self-same bridge.

'Sure isn't that a strange thing to come into my mind? When I saw the face of them at the accident I had no doubt at all that they were the self-same people.'

## Wraith Warning from Butte to Inishowen

Michael McGuinness was a well-known and well-liked historian in Derry. A few years ago when I was chatting to him I mentioned that I was collecting ghost stories. 'I have one,' he said and he told me this story.

When his grandfather John's father died, he left the farm to John's older brother. The farm was not big enough to keep both, so, like many other younger sons in those days, John went off to work in Scotland. He worked hard and saved hard and at a ceilidh one night he met a lovely young Scottish girl by the name of Celia Kelly and they fell in love. Celia was from Greenock and she was much taken with John.

Soon they married and set up home together. In time, they had three children and although things were going well for them in Scotland John had a longing to return to Inishowen. It seemed that his wish would be granted for letters began

*Wraith from Butte to Inishowen.*

to arrive advising him to come home. It seemed that his brother had little interest in the farm and wanted him to take it over. He agreed to do this and within a short time they had packed their possessions and returned to Ireland with their children. They settled in Lug, a quiet townland outside Moville.

But the farm was a bit run-down and they had very little money to spare. John realised that he would have to earn some extra money to build the farm up again. At that time, many young Irish men were going abroad to work and he heard that there was good money to be made by hard workers willing to go to the copper mines in Butte, Montana. He and his wife discussed what he should do and although they knew it would be hard they agreed that it was the best solution for them at that time. If he worked hard then they might be able to turn things around within a year. Celia assured her husband

that although she would miss him she would manage until he returned. The cottage was comfortable and she would be able to put the money he would send home from America to good use.

The couple wrote to each other regularly. Celia told him about the children and eagerly awaited his replies. Life in Lug was lonely enough for a young woman who had been reared in a big city in Scotland. Although she knew that John was working hard, she and the children missed him and she had it in mind to ask him to come home. She thought that they would manage somehow. She was determined that her husband would return to a warm and welcoming home, but fate took a hand in their lives and it was not to be.

On 9 June 1917, she was going about her normal daily chores, lighting the fire, cooking breakfast and cleaning up. When she finished washing up in the kitchen, she picked up the basin and went to the half-door to empty the water. What she saw outside took her by surprise, but her joy turned to shock and fright. Her husband was standing outside at the gate, but she soon realised that there was something eerie about his stance. He stood very still and looked straight at her, but his eyes seemed blank, as if he was staring straight through her. Then he turned his back as if to walk away.

Slowly she put the basin down and opened the door, but as she walked towards him the child's cry distracted her. When she looked back to the gate again there was no one there. She rushed towards it and looked up and down the road but it was empty. There was no one to be seen.

Returning quickly to the house, she felt a terrible dread come upon her. With nervous fingers she lit a blessed candle, took out her rosary beads and prayed for her husband's safety, but she was overcome by a terrible premonition that something had happened to him. When she shared her fears with John's family and their neighbours, they laughed and told her that she was being fanciful and foolish, but she couldn't settle her mind and in her heart she knew that something was wrong.

She waited and worried for the next few days, always wondering what might have happened. On the third day the postman came to her house with a telegram. Before she opened it she knew what it would say: it would tell her that her husband was dead.

She was right. The telegram informed her that her husband had been among the 167 miners killed in the Speculator Mine explosion in Butte, Montana. The time of his death was the same time that she had seen him standing at their gate.

It was the worst mining disaster in Montana's history. The fire broke out in the lower levels of the mine, caused by a broken power cable that carried electricity to the underground pumps. Lower levels of the mine quickly filled with smoke and gas. John's body was the first of the dead miners to be taken from the mine.

John and Celia's families were shocked at the death, but they were also perplexed and amazed that she had had a premonition long before she knew the facts of her husband's death.

John's grave is in Butte Montana and his name appears on the 'Granite Mountain Memorial Plaques'.

Celia died not long afterwards, leaving four orphaned children, three boys and a girl, in Inishowen. Her grandson Michael, now deceased, was convinced that there had been a transference of love, thought and feeling between his grandfather and his grandmother at that time.

## The Inch Banshee

It is well known that the banshee follows certain families. I interviewed a storyteller in Inch called Bertie Bryce several times over the years and one of his true stories concerned a visit of a banshee to his mother-in-law.

Her name was Annie Fleming and she married John Galbraith. John changed his surname to Galbraith Fleming in order to inherit an aunt's estate. He was known as Jack on the island and they were blessed with one daughter Ina, who married Bertie.

Annie was in bed with the flu and Jack was upstairs attending to her when a few of his friends, old James Boyle and Joe Hegarty, came in. He called to them that he would be down in a minute and he proceeded to make his wife comfortable. He fluffed up her pillows, straightened the bedclothes and gave her something to drink. Before he went downstairs, he put more coal on the fire because the bedroom tended to be cold and asked her if she would be all right. She assured him that she would.

'Go on down to your friends. Sure, if I need you, I'll call.'

She heard Jack's footsteps as he descended the stairs because in those days the floors and stairs wouldn't have been carpeted and the noise carried. He would have been about three steps from the bottom when a *sí* (banshee) came 'sliping' across the landing with a strange shuffling gait and rattled the bedroom door. Annie looked across and watched the handle go down, then up, followed by the door opening.

She cowered in bed, holding the bedclothes tight to her chin. She heard the strange sound of the *sí* shuffling across the room. 'It was as if she was dragging her foot,' she explained later, 'and the sound stopped when this *sí* came to the fireplace. I watched the poker rise into the air and then all I saw was a hand moving it in and out of the fire, poking at it and making a terrible amount of noise.'

Annie roared with fright and squealed as loud as she could for Jack, who came running up the stairs and burst into the room.

'In the name of God, Annie,' he said, 'what's the matter with you?'

Sure, he couldn't get a coherent word out of her. She just continued to screech. He could see that she was in some sort of a trance and he shook her to rouse her from it.

'In the name of God, Annie,' he cried out again, 'what ails ye?'

By this time, James and Joe, the men who were waiting downstairs, took the stairs two at a time and came to a stop at the door. It was an awful shock for them to see this normally quiet woman in such a state, her eyes wide and her body trembling. She pointed to the fire and started then to tell about the *sí*. Jack nodded to them to go back downstairs. When he was alone with her, she took his arm and described what she had seen and heard.

'I heard her "slipe" across the floor and then I saw a hand – nothing else – lift the poker and start raking up the fire. Ye must have heard her for she dragged that foot behind her.'

'Where is she now, Annie? Sure ye must have been imagining it.' Jack was distraught.

'I don't know,' cried Annie. 'Maybe she disappeared out the window. I don't know but she was there and then there was just her hand, poking away at the fire.'

Jack went over to the fire and lifted the poker. Although it had been stuck among the glowing embers it was icy cold to the touch. He knew then that something strange had happened and went back to Annie to pacify her. When she calmed down and dozed off, he went to his friends downstairs, where they held an inquest into Annie's strange behaviour.

'Was she raving?' they asked.

'Raving! Not a bit of it. She's as sensible as I am and I believe her. If she says she heard the *sí* with that shuffling gait then she heard it. I've no doubt about that at all for my Annie doesn't imagine things.'

His friends had been ready to dismiss the episode as a hysterical outburst from a sick woman but when he mentioned the strange dragging gait they looked at one another and Jack saw shock and recognition in their eyes.

Joe Hegarty said, 'There was only one woman that that sliping gait could have belonged to and that was a woman called Mary Peoples who lived in this house before Annie was married. But sure, Annie wouldn't have met her or even known her.'

He went on to say that when she got older and was no longer able to look after herself, her daughter brought her over to where she lived near Glasgow.

'But sure, that woman must be dead years ago,' said Boyle. 'She's bound to be for if she was alive she'd be near a hundred.'

The next morning a wire came to Durnin's of the post office. 'To whom it may concern, Mary Peoples died last night in Scotland.'

They heard afterwards that Mary had dementia and had wandered out. Her daughter and grandchildren searched high and low for her but she was nowhere to be found. Eventually they came upon her where she had collapsed near an old shed in the back garden. It was a cold evening with a light fall of snow and Mary was in a bad way. They managed to carry her back to the house and sent for the doctor but she was 98 years old and feeble and she passed away at 8.45 p.m. that night.

It was at that exact time that Annie had experienced the manifestation of the *sí* in her room. That was the one and only time a banshee appeared to Annie.

# 3

# HAUNTED PLACES

## The Ghost of the Old Eel Weir

The old eel weir at Cliffe, Ballyshannon, was one of three such weirs on the River Erne. Right from the time of the O'Donnells down to the First World War, Ballyshannon had a prosperous trade in eels and salmon. Before the time of railways and steamers, most of the salmon and eels were salted and cured in buildings on the Mall before beginning their export journey to England and the Mediterranean.

*Eel Weir.*

A man named Scanlon and another man were employed as waterkeepers on the eel weirs at Cliffe. They were men who were well able for the job. They had worked together for over the ten years. They took the watch in turns and usually the nights passed without incident, apart from a few run-ins with poachers.

One night, however, was different. After supper, at around 11.30 p.m., Scanlon's fellow waterkeeper went off for his sleep and Scanlon continued to keep watch. The night was quiet and the full moon illuminated the water of the River Erne as it flowed by. This was a favourite time for Scanlon as the world was at rest and he could smoke his pipe and contemplate.

As the town clock struck twelve, he heard the door open behind him and someone entered. Startled, he jumped from his chair, knocking it to the floor. He turned to see who had interrupted his reverie. It was not a poacher, as he had feared, but a woman. She stood holding the latch of the door.

She was tall and fair-haired with a long thin face. Her clothes were stylish and her neat brown boots shone but her brown worsted woollen gown was old-fashioned.

'Who are you?' cried Scanlon. 'What do you want?'

To his own ears his voice sounded almost shrill. His hands suddenly lost feeling and his pipe fell. She did not speak but stood looking at him for two minutes and then smiled, showing one prominent tooth. The smile did not reach her eyes. As Scanlon moved forward, she backed out of the weir house without turning and the door closed quietly after her.

Though very frightened and confused, Scanlon rushed to open the door. The moon was obscured behind a cloud and when it cleared he could see that there was no one outside. He knew it was impossible to get to the weir house across the treacherous river without the aid of a boat. How had the woman done so?

He backed into the house again and once safely inside he bolted the door and woke his companion. At first his friend did not believe him, but seeing Scanlon's distress he listened and then took it upon himself to investigate outside.

There was nothing to be seen and no one to be found, but he knew that Scanlon was not a man given to strange imaginings and asked him again to recount what he experienced.

The following morning when Scanlon was going home he met the old man who had once done the same job and was now retired. Scanlon debated with himself whether he should tell him what had happened. Although he felt a trifle foolish, he asked the old man if he had ever seen anything strange at the weir house.

'Tell me what you saw,' the old man said.

Scanlon told him, deliberately leaving out some details. When he had finished, the old man described the same woman, filling in the missing details. Scanlon was then absolutely convinced that the appearance had not been a figment of his imagination.

The old man went on to say that the lady had appeared to him on the same date twenty years before and that something had made him rise early today and go to the weir.

'You see, young Scanlon, my predecessor in the weir house had the same woman appear to him and he told me that this woman was murdered there in a foul and brutal manner and always appeared at intervals of twenty years, at the same time, twelve o'clock. It wasn't your imagination and I charge you to pass on this information to the next water keeper when you retire. I'm only sorry I didn't set out to see you last night and delayed till now. But there it is. That's the story, believe it or believe it not.'

## The Ghost of Owencarrow

On a wild and stormy winter's night,
The little train did steam,
Adown past Kilmacrennan
And Lurgy's purling stream.
She passed along down through the gap,
The Owencarrow she passed by,
Until she reached the hills of Doe,
Beneath an angry sky.

A sudden gust came from above
Two carriages were swept o'er,
Three passengers there met their death,
Leaving hearts both sad and sore.
One other soul did pass away,
Her race on earth is done
She died in Letterkenny
At the rising of the dawn.

(D. Hay. This ballad was written to commemorate the Viaduct disaster at Owencarrow.)

*Owencarrow Viaduct disaster. (Courtesy of Donegal Railway Restoration Society)*

When the Londonderry and Lough Swilly Railway Company built a railway track in Donegal, little did they think that it would be remembered for the terrible disaster that claimed four lives on the Owencarrow Viaduct on 31 January 1925. The place of the tragedy has reputedly been haunted ever since then.

The Owencarrow River winds its way through the hills of Donegal and when the railway was built it had to cross the valley on its way to Creeslough and thence onto the coast. The track was an extension 3ft gauge line that ran almost 50 miles from Letterkenny, encircling the Donegal Mountains right to Burtonport.

It was a joint venture between the British government and the Londonderry and Lough Swilly Railway Company but in an effort to save on the cost of construction, it skirted by miles some small towns that it was meant to serve. The extension line was the government's attempt to alleviate the terrible poverty of north-west Donegal and it was a godsend to the people living in these barren Gaeltacht areas.

Ireland at that time was famous for its new viaducts over the most inhospitable of land and crossing the Owencarrow River and glen was certainly a challenge because of the mountainous and boggy terrain. The railway track had to descend to the bog, which meant that there was a very steep incline. On the far side of the bog there was solid rock where a narrow cutting had to be dynamited to allow the train to go down onto the clearway.

Viaducts also had to be constructed over low-lying land at Barnes Gap and Faymore. The Owencarrow Viaduct rested on high granite pillars. After the disaster, local people said that the foundations had been built on 'sheep's wool', an accusation that was not disputed.

The line opened for traffic in 1903 and very soon became an integral part of the lives of the Gaeltacht people. It served them well, especially the emigrants who went to work digging potatoes in Scotland or toiling in deep tunnels or building roads in England. Many of those who went farther afield to America and Canada began their journey at the small stations along the L&LS Railway Company line. Many youngsters who were 'hired' at the hiring fairs returned joyfully by train at the end of their tenure in the bigger towns of Strabane, Letterkenny and Derry. In the twenty years that the line was open before Owencarrow Viaduct disaster, there were only two fatalities reported. Following both fatalities the line was the subject of enquiries over its safety and operation. The Derry Chamber of Commerce stated that 'defective construction and inadequate and unsuitable equipment' were at the root of the line's many ills.

From time to time, rumours flew about concerning strange sightings on the line. Drivers said that they were almost certain that someone or something strange was walking on the line at times. When they applied the brakes to slow down and moved carefully to the spot where they thought they had seen something, the line was always clear and empty. Still, there were too many 'unexplained' sightings to ignore on that particular part of the line between Barnesmore and Creeslough.

On Friday 31 January 1925, a mixed passenger and goods train, Engine No. 14, pulled out of Derry at 5.30 p.m. with fourteen passengers, eight goods wagons and two bread vans. When the train left Letterkenny the number of passengers had swollen to thirty-six. As it headed west the winds began to rise and at Barnes Gap the driver remarked that the wind was a 'terrible bad' one. Soon there were gusts of up to 120mph, the train was shaking on the line and the carriages began to sway with each strong gust.

According to John Hannigan, the fireman, the wind was so strong that they had to apply the brakes hard in order to stop the train from being pushed down the slope too quickly.

The driver was Bob McGuinness, a man with thirteen years' experience on the line. He slowed the train to 10mph as it approached the 440-yard long viaduct, knowing that this particular crossing was extremely dangerous in bad weather. He noticed only one thing out of the ordinary; he thought he saw a vague shadow as he peered through the small porthole windows at the track on the viaduct ahead. He approached the high viaduct cautiously but when he was scarcely 60 yards from the Creeslough side a ferocious gust of wind smashed one carriage against the parapet. It lifted the carriage next to the engine right off the rails. The driver immediately applied the vacuum brake to stop the train but the last carriage, having been lifted off, pulled the other wagons halfway over the protective parapet of the bridge. One carriage somersaulted onto its roof and splintered 'like matchwood', according to John Hannigan. The occupants of that carriage were hurled through the smashed roof to the rocky ravine forty feet below, where broken masonry rained down on them. Three people died instantly.

Johnny jumped down from the engine, but there was no space for anyone else to move past him. Imagine his shock when a man in a cloak rushed by shouting, 'This is terrible! This is terrible!' before he vanished into the darkness.

Johnny was absolutely sure that no passenger would have been able to squeeze between the rocky cutting and the engine to pass him since the space was barely wide enough for the train. That experience of someone passing him haunted John Hannigan all his life because it simply didn't make sense to him.

Who or what was this strange form coming out of the dark storm dressed all in black? It was something he didn't dare to think about as he ran all the way to Creeslough 3 miles away to raise the alarm. It must have been an awful journey for him for the viaduct was in the middle of nowhere and with the rain was pelting down and the wind still gusting ferociously it took him over an hour to fetch help. Even then, it was almost impossible for the rescuers to reach the train except along the railway track.

Bob McGuinness and Johnny Hannigan questioned themselves. Was this black shadow the spirit that they sensed on the track beforehand? Had it been trying to warn them of the impending disaster?

Other people said that a man approached the stricken carriages and helped to free the injured and when help arrived from Creeslough he was nowhere to be seen. He had disappeared. One witness described him as a tall man dressed in black.

Another woman reported that on one occasion several years after the disaster, her mother and at least four other people saw an old woman who walked to the spot where the train crash had happened and although there is no bridging track and only the pillars standing, she appeared to walk across the viaduct and follow the line over the hill. This woman was dressed in clothes from the 1920s and was wearing a headscarf. She paused on the other side and was observed holding rosary beads and blessing herself.

At the inquest, the jury recorded the bravery of two men: James 'The Post' McFadden of Kilfad and Pat 'Paddy Rua' McFadden of Terlin. These men rescued two women from a dangling carriage, which was suspended only by its chains. The complete jury added that 'if a properly constructed rail had been carried along the whole length of the viaduct, from cutting to cutting, and without an intervening gap, no lives would have been lost'. They exonerated the driver, fireman and guard from any blame whatsoever.

The people who lost their lives were Philip and Sarah Boyle from Arranmore Island, Una Mulligan from Falcarragh and Neil Duggan from Meenbunowen, Creeslough, whose home was only a stone's throw from the crash.

The viaduct was repaired and the line continued to serve the area for another sixteen years and although the last passenger train journey from Letterkenny to Burtonport took place on June 1941 the tragedy is still fresh in the minds of local people and stories of ghostly sightings abound.

## The Kinnego Blacksmith

Between 1534 and 1603, there was a Crown policy of plantation involving the arrival of thousands of English and Scottish Protestant settlers. They established themselves throughout the country, particularly in the provinces of Ulster and Munster. They did this principally by confiscating the lands previously owned by the Gaelic clans and Hiberno-Norman dynasties. These people were consequently displaced and initially there was a series of Irish military campaigns against the invaders, who were certainly not given a free rein.

The clans fought back and in their fearless fighting they sometimes regained ground but they needed weapons to help them in their fight against their oppressors. One smith in particular became famous for his skill making swords, pikes and other warlike instruments. Once word of his superior weaponry spread, he found that his life was in danger.

Orders were issued to remove him by any means. The invading forces believed that if he was killed, their enemies would be less successful as they would no longer have access to a supply of superb weapons made from the finest metal. He was driven to move from place to place to avoid being captured by the English. In each place, he set up a smithy and continued to make and supply the local warriors with their weapons of war.

Eventually he believed that he had found a place that was well hidden from the invaders. It was not too far from the sea, deep in the woods at the foot of Crocknasmug Hill. There he spent his days and nights creating a splendid armoury for the fighting men of the area. To muffle the sound of his hammer on the anvil he covered the smithy with thick sods that also acted as camouflage against the woodland backdrop.

Slowly but surely, the English advanced northwards and their scouts, believed to be local informers, led them to his hiding place. They watched while he worked and listened to the dulled sound of the hammer on the anvil as he formed his perfect ironware.

When evening came they charged from the woods and brutally attacked the blacksmith. When he was only half-conscious, they tied him to a huge oak tree and made him watch as they scattered his tools and stole the weapons he had already made. The Crown soldiers whooped in delight and waved the swords high when their officers distributed the weapons to them. They demolished the smithy and scattered the red-hot embers around to make a bonfire of it. The blacksmith watched them drink and fall about as they danced around the fire, yelling triumphantly.

When the flames died down they took him to his anvil and placed his neck upon it and with one mighty stroke from one of his own magnificent long swords they beheaded him. Not content with that, the maddened soldiers took his head and unceremoniously stuck it on the top of a pike. They left it there as a lesson for all of the defeated men of the area so they would understand what would happen to those who defied the Crown. The local people were appalled at the lack of dignity with which the invaders treated the smith's body but there was little they could do.

Such was the loyalty to the smith and the people's outrage at his martyrdom that at a later time a village sprang up near that spot and was given the name of *Cionn na Gabha* (Head of the Smith), later anglicised to Kinnego.

However, that is not the end of the story. According to Maghtochair's *Inishowen*, 'though his life-blood was shed by the incensed soldiery still his hearth was not extinguished, nor his patriotic labours concluded. Ever since that, from night-fall till morning, in the calm of summer or the angry tempests of winter, the ruddy glow of his fire can be distinctly seen by every inhabitant of that wild mountainous valley.'

He goes on to say that even at a distance of 2 miles, every night he watched the recurrence of the scene of 'the iron borne from the fire to the sounding anvil', but because of the distance he was unable to hear the sound of the hammer striking the anvil or the bellows blowing the embers into flames.

Maghtochair was adamant that this was no imaginative 'Will-o'-the-Wisp' theory because the fiery glow was too red, steady and unchanging for that. 'He is engaged in the manufacture of arms for the enchanted land of Elagh; and from his dexterity and his close attention to business he will be ready with such a supply of needle-guns for them as will enable them to enter the lists with the best military tacticians of the day.'

And so the story has lived on.

been murdered with a pickaxe by an elderly couple who gave him shelter in their old farmhouse nearby. They killed him for his belongings and they tried to hide their crime by stuffing him in his pack after emptying it of the goods. Unfortunately for them, he was too tall. Undaunted, they cut off his legs at the knees, wrapped them in a pickle of hay, put his body into the pack and buried him.

Legend says he was buried among the roots of a tree. He came back for vengeance as a gruesome ghost that walked about on the stumps of his legs and tormented his killers to their dying day. The legend tells us that the ghost went over the bridge and there is bridge near the brae.

## The Legend of Stumpy's Brae

The steep slope known as Stumpy's Brae lies between Craighadoes and Lifford. Mrs Cecil Frances Alexander, wife of the Church of Ireland Bishop of Derry, was the author of the well-known hymns 'Once in Royal David's City' and 'All Things Bright and Beautiful'. She preserved the legend of Stumpy in poetry form and is reputed to be the author of this version of the ballad, which bore her initials and 1844, the year in which it was composed.

There are indications that she was revising and editing an older poem. There can be little doubt that Mrs Alexander was not the original author of the poem and the poem was made to conserve an oral Ulster-Scot's tradition.

In the 1700s, there was a pedlar man by the name of Tom the Toiler, who was, according to this poem, buried in a small brae between what used to be Joshua Galbraith's house and the road. He had

Heard ye no tell o' Stympy's Brae
Sit doone, sit down, young friend,
I'll make your flesh to creep this night
And your hair to stand on end.
Young man, it's hard to strive wi' sin
And the hardest strife o' a'
Is when the greed o' gain comes in
And drives God's grace awa'.
O, it's quick to do, but it's long to rue
When the punishment comes at last
And we'd gi' the whole world to undo
    the deed
That deed that's gone and past.
Over yon strip of meadowland
And over the bintie bright
Mark ye well where a fir-tree stands
Beside yon gable white.
O, I mind it weel, in my younger days
When the story yet was rife
There dwelt within that lovely place
A farmer man and his wife.
They sat together all alone
That blessed autumn night
When the trees without and hedge and
    stone

Were white in the sweet moonlight.
The boys and girls had all gone down
A wee tae the blacksmith's wake
When passed my on by the window small
Ad gi'ed the door a shake.
The man he up and opened the door,
And when he had spoken a bit,
A pedlar man stepped in to the floor
Down tumbled the pack he bore right
    heavy pack it was.
'God save us a',' says the wife wi' a smile,
'But yours is a thriving trade.'
'Ay, ay, I've wandered many a mile,
And plenty I have made.'
'Well, come on in and sit ye doon,
Would ye like a wee cup of tae?
Sure put your bag agin that wall.
It's not gonnie run away.'
The man sat on by the dull fire flame
When the pedlar went to his rest,
Close to his ear the Devil came,
And slipped into his breast.
He looked at his wife by the dim firelight
And she was as bad as he.
'Could we no' murder yon man tonight?'
'Aye, could we no'?' ready quo' she.
He took the pick-axe without a word
Where it stood behind the door.
As he passed it into the sleeper he stirred
And never wakened more.
'He's dead,' says the auld wan coming back,
'What o' the corpse, my dear?'
'We'll bury him snug in his ain bit pack,
Never ye mind the loss o' the sack
I've taken out a' the gear.'
'The packs ower short by two quid span,
And what'll we do?' quo' he.
'And you're a doited thoughtful man,
We'll soon cuit him off at the knee.'
They shortened the corpse, and they
    packed him tight
Wi' his legs in a pickle o' hay.
Over the burn in the sweet moonlight,
They carried him to this brae.

The shovelled a hole right speddily
And they laid him on his back
'A right pair are ye,' quo' the pedlar,
He sitting bolt upright in his pack.
'Ye though ye'd lay me snugly here
Where none should know my station
But I'll haunt ye far, and I'll haunt ye near,
Father and son, with terror and fear,
    to the nineteenth generation.'
The two were sitting the very next night
When the wee bit dog began to cower
And they knew by the pale blue firelight
That the evil one had power.
It had just struck nine, just nine o' the clock,
That hour when the man lay dead,
Where there came to the outer door a knock,
And a heavy, heavy tread,
The auld man's head swam round and round,
The woman's head gang freeze,
T'was not like a natural sound,
But like someone stomping over the ground
On the bones o' his raw bare knees.
In through the door like a sough of air,
And stomp! Stomp! Stomp! Around the twa'
Wi' his bloody head, and his knee bone bare
They had maist tae die awa'.
The wife's black locks ere the morn grew
    white,
They say, as the mountain snows,
The man was as straight as a staff that night
But he stooped as the morning arose.
Still day-by-day as the clock struck nine,
In the house where they did the sin,
The wee bit dog began to whine
And the ghost came clatterin' in.
Wan night, there was a fearful flood,
Three days and nights the skies had poured
And white wi' foam and black wi' wind
The burn in fury roared.
Quo' she, 'Guid man ye need nae turn sae
    pale.'
Says she in the dim fire light,
'The stumpy canna cross the burn
He'll no' be here the nicht.

For it up the Jinn and it 'ower the bank
And it's up to the meadow ridge'
But the stumpy he came harplin' in,
Gave the wife a slap on the chin
'Sure came round by the bridge.'
And stump, stump, stump to his ploys
    again
Over the stools and chairs,
Ye'd surely hae thought ten men and women
Were dancing there in pairs.
To a foreign land they went
But sure what can flee from
His appointed punishment?
The ship swam over the water clear
We' the help o' an eastern breeze
But the very first sound on the wide,
    smooth deck,
That fell on their ears, was the tappin' o'
    them bare knees.
Out in the woods of wild America
Their weary feet they set,
But stumpy was the first they say,
and haunted them to their dying day.
And he follows their children yet,
This is the story o' Stumpy's Brae
And the murderer's fearful fate.
Young friend, your face is turned that way,
You'll be ganging the night that gate.
Yell ken it well, through the few fir trees
The house where they were wont to dwell
If ye meet ane there as daylight flees,
Stumping about on the banes o' his knees
It'll just be Stumpy himsel'.

## The Lost Man of Urris

Dunaff Hill in Inishowen is a sombre peak facing the Atlantic Ocean. Far beneath it, caves pierce the dark cliffs and echo with the waves that rise and ebb with the tides.

There is a story told about a man from Urris, the area between Dunaff and Leenan, who climbed down the rocky cliff to gather limpets and mussels. It was Lent, a time when people abstained from meat, and it was an old spring tradition that limpets gathered during that season were good bait for fish. The men would be thankful to have a catch of fish, but, failing that, their families could eat shellfish and be glad of the harvest of the sea.

The man reached the beach and noticed that the tide had receded far out. He decided to enter one of the caves when he saw that there was an abundance of limpets clinging to the rocks beyond the entrance. He soon filled one of the bags he had brought and eagerly worked to fill the other one, but so intent was he on his task that he forgot to keep an eye on the tide. Only when the cold water swirled around his feet did he realise what a perilous situation he was in. To his dismay, there was no way out at that time for the rough waters were already at the mouth of the cave and within moments they had cut off any hope of escape.

As the waves began to sweep closer and higher, he retreated further and further into the cavern, desperately seeking some place of safety, but there did not seem to be anywhere out of reach of the surging sea. When he had almost given up hope, he saw a ledge above the high-water mark and he began to clamber up to the ledge in a panic while the icy water snapped at his heels.

When he was safely settled, he took stock of his situation and saw that a smaller cave lay beyond the ledge. He realised that he was indeed fortunate. He lay down the bags filled with the shellfish he had gathered and huddled in the near darkness to await the turning of the tide. He tried not to dwell on his predicament and his own stupidity and worried about his family, who would be concerned when he didn't return as expected.

Meanwhile, his family waited at home, but when a terrible storm began to rattle the windows their anxiety turned to fear for his safety. As they always did in times of trouble, they turned to prayer. The night was long and when the thunder rolled and the lightening flashed his wife sent the children to bed. She kept vigil until dawn, but when the howling wind and rain had not abated, she grew increasingly fearful and began to walk the floor with her rosary beads in her hands, praying that her husband was safe.

In the morning, she went to her neighbour's house to let them know what had happened. Soon they gathered in her home but the weather conditions were so terrible that it seemed that there was very little hope for the man. Too many men had died in the sea and the small community braced itself for the worst news about their friend.

Most believed that he had somehow lost his footing and tumbled into the sea for the spring tide was higher and more ferocious than usual. They searched for him along the shore, expecting each day that they might find his mangled body, but as the weeks passed they gave up hope and they mourned with his family.

While his family and neighbours were searching, the man, imprisoned by the high spring tides and knowing that entering the water meant sure death, resigned himself to the fact that he was unable to escape from the cave. He ate what he could find. Sometimes stray birds flew into the cave and he devised a means of catching them. He forced himself to eat the raw flesh of birds, fish and shellfish to stay alive. In this way, he managed to survive.

*The Lost Man of Urris.*

It was near the end of March when the awful weather calmed and the water fell to a low enough level for him to escape. Emaciated and feeble, he made his way home, but when he reached his house, such was the shock of his family when they saw this 'strange' man at their door that his wife fainted. A neighbour came running and after some time and questioning was able to verify that this was indeed the woman's husband come back from the dead. The family immediately invited friends and neighbours to celebrate his homecoming. Unfortunately, the feast in his honour was his undoing.

When they served him the steaming hot, tasty food that he had dreamed of during his time in the cave, he ate like a man demented, unaware that his constitution was sorely changed. His body was so unused to the rich food that he took ill that very night and died.

There never was such a wake in that parish as there was for this man who had died once and been mourned twice.

Soon after his death, rumours began to circulate about his spirit wandering along the shore and disappearing into the cave once more. People started to hear the low moaning of a ghost rising in the wind and the locals stayed safely in their houses whenever they heard it.

No one ever dared to enter that cave again.

# 4

# PHANTOM PIPERS' CAVES

The legend of the piper's ghost droning on his pipes in a cave or at a rock is a common one throughout Ireland. Some say that the sounds are caused by the wind entering the cave and making the sound of musical notes as it swirls and curls through the crannies and the cracks. Disbelievers deny this and say that such sweet music could not possibly be made accidently. When the musical notes seem to float along fast-flowing streams they are known as the 'Devil's Mill' and locals are always cautious about crossing the water when the sound can be heard.

## The Piper's Cave, Ballintra

Often the lonely wail of the pipes is heard swirling from the Piper's Cave. This is one of a series of caves in a curious ravine called 'The Pullans', through which the River Blackwater flows in the Brownhall Demesne close to the village of Ballintra, County Donegal.

The story goes that a young man from the demesne was getting married and, as was the tradition then, everyone from the area was invited. A wedding feast would not be complete without a musician, so Condy McGrorty, the best piper in the area, was invited to play. The people ate and drank their fill and the merriment spilled into the wee small hours. Poor Condy was plied with drink to keep the music going. After a while he was so full of drink that he didn't know if he was coming or going. He staggered outside for a breath of fresh air and wandered down the path that led to the caves.

Inside the hall people were singing and carousing and they forgot all about poor Condy until the groom called for more music. They searched the hall and when they could not find him, a few men – the worse for drink, it must be said – went outside to look for him. A full moon lit up the cliffs and the sea and in the calm night air they heard the faint strains of the music floating towards them. They followed the sound down to the caves and so sweet was the music that they halted and sat on the rocks to listen. When it finally stopped, two of the men ventured inside to check if Condy was all right and to pass on the groom's request for more music.

They had only been gone a few minutes when the men outside heard shouting and the thumping of feet on the rocks. The two men who had braved the caves came running out, jabbering about it being haunted. When they quieted down they all listened and they heard strange, echoing, ethereal noises. As the music rose and fell, they found themselves being drawn into the cave. When it stopped for a moment, the enchantment was broken. They took to their heels and ran back to the Brownhall House, declaring that they would never set foot inside that cave again.

Poor Condy McGrorty was never ever seen again, but the sound of his pipes still emanates from the cave on moonlit nights when the air is still. It is said that if you venture near the mouth of the cave you too could become so enchanted by the haunting music that you would wander in and suffer the same fate as Condy.

In 1929, the bones of a human skeleton were found in the Piper's Cave by a party of botanists. The bones were sent to London where 'they were deemed – for an unrecorded reason – to be between 400 and 600 years old' (Marion Dowd, *Archeology of Ireland*, p.61).

There are many stories about the ghostly sounds that haunt the Piper's Hole. One local piper tells of a piper in the nineteenth century who was trying to make an underground journey through the caves between Maghera and Glencolmcille. The tune he was heard playing was a hiterto unknown air now known as 'The Piper in the Cave March'. This was the last one he played before he was eaten by a wild beast (Padraig 18/9/2004 at The Session, according to *Irish Ghosts: A Ghost Hunter's Guide* by Peter Underwood).

For years the mournful sounds of the Uileann pipes were reported intermittently and no rational explanation was ever discovered. Witnesses include John Hogan, Jessie Matthews, Robert Aickman and Dr Peter Hilton-Rowe.

## Poll an Phíobaire, Clonmany

Clonmany is a small village on the west side of the Inishowen Peninsula. If you follow the stream at the edge of the village you will eventually come to Binion beach. There is a wild beauty about this lonely stretch of shore, to which high tides have made access almost impossible in the last few years.

Binion Hill overlooks the beach and on winter evenings when waves sweep in from Malin Head, the most northerly part of the island of Ireland, the hill stands strong. One of the infamous Famine walls runs from the bottom to the top of the hill. Starving men built this wall. Their only hope of staying alive was to work for the overlords who demanded that they pull, haul and lift the heavy rocks from the hillside to build a wall that was going nowhere. Many men died from the effort and their wives and children suffered in the workhouses.

It is no wonder that local legends abound, detailing strange and eerie happenings, particularly on evenings when the raw, sharp northerly wind whips the sand into a vicious frenzy. It is then that those lost souls who perished on lonely Binion Hill are said to wander on the beach and dunes and the faint music of the pipes is heard above the screeching storm. Locals will tell you that there is a cave under Binion Hill where a lonely piper once sheltered from a wintry storm.

He was playing his favourite air, 'Girls will be old women before I return', and was so intent on his music that he wandered too far into the cave. That was the last that was seen of him but the sound of his music is still carried on the wind and so the cave became known as *Poll an Phíobaire* (The Piper's Cave).

## The Piper's Cave, Fanad

Imagine a lonely beach stretching along the coast of the Fanad Peninsula in north Donegal. There, on dark nights when the clouds hide the moon, a sad and plaintive drone drifts from the Piper's Cave that stretches under Lehadan Hill near the townland of Killycolman.

In the raw wilderness above the cave on the south-west slope of the hill, three tall standing stones overlook the coastal waters and it can seem as if they are listening to the strains of the melody. The moonlight occasionally breaks through the cloud cover and highlights a squared standing stone. On the face of the huge stone a cross is deeply gouged, as if in remembrance of the people who died in the cave below.

Locals suspect that these stones are connected with the legend of the Piper's Cave in some mysterious way for it was on such a night that the men, women and children of the Killycolman area were murdered by the marauding O'Donnell clan. Indeed, the legend is not complimentary to the O'Donnells because it tells of how, shortly after they had settled in Rathmullan, they began to ravish the county northward as far as the wild Atlantic Ocean.

It during one of these incursions that the terrified people rushed to the cave and hid there in the hope that the O'Donnells would not discover them. However, despite their attempts to hide, the O'Donnells found them and set about smothering men, women and children without mercy. Satisfied that they had eliminated all of them, they built a high bonfire to feast and celebrate their victory.

They did not realise that they had overlooked one man. He was the piper. He had gone so far into the cave that he escaped the fate of his fellows. When he emerged at daylight, he was so sickened by what he saw that he lost his senses and since then his ghost has been wandering about, bewailing the fate of his friends in the only way that he can; by playing a requiem for them. So at times his pipes can be heard along the shore, even miles from the cave mouth.

A man near Curraghkeel was adamant that he often heard the drone of the pipes under his farm. He was not the only one to recount the same story. Another man who lived near Oughterlinn also heard the sad sound of the pipes.

*The Piper's Cave, Fanad and its three standing stones.*

# 5

# OTHERWORLD HAUNTINGS

## Archie's Craw

There is a place at Ballymaghgarey outside Moville in Inishowen known as Archie's Craw. It was named after Archie McDonald, who was with the first batch of planters to come over from England to settle in Donegal. A craw is a place where pigs were reared or where sheep were penned.

Archie was not married at that time and he often went down to a place called the Bens near Tremone Bay. The Bens were high cliffs and below them was a big black rock half-covered with seaweed and limpets. Archie was of a mind to gather the seaweed and dry it out for dulse, but when he was still some distance away from the rock he noticed something moving.

When he got nearer his heart nearly stopped beating for there, sitting on the rock, was a beautiful mermaid combing her long blonde hair. Careful not to make too much noise, he made his way down to the rock and began to talk to her. She didn't seem afraid and listened to Archie as he talked. She had a laugh that tinkled and sounded as sweet as drops of water on a shell.

As he spoke, he tried not to look at the shimmering blue tailfin, which she had instead of legs. He knew from the tales that his mother and grandmother had told that when a human hand touched a mermaid's tailfin she would become human and also that if she touched the fin with her own hand she would immediately revert to being a mermaid. As she looked out to sea, Archie gently touched the fin and it came away in his hand like shimmering aqua-blue satin. He concealed it in his coat. When she turned around, she spoke to him, asking where he lived.

'I'll show you,' said Archie and with that he took her back home. He was so madly in love with her that within a few days he went the minister and persuaded him to solemnise the marriage. But he always felt that if she got the opportunity she would go back to the sea so he hid the tailfin in a hole in the wall in a barn where he thought no one would find it.

Archie and Mara lived very happily together and in time brought two children into the world. Archie was the envy of his friends because he had such a beautiful and biddable wife. She never objected to anything that Archie had a mind to do, unlike some of the local wives, who had a hard time keeping their husbands in line.

On Fair Day, Archie went into Moville as usual, but he stayed longer than he should have. It seems that he met two men and went into the pub for a few drinks. He returned home well inebriated and when he arrived at the house he was surprised to see the children still up. Usually his wife had them in bed by eight o'clock.

'Where's your mammy?' he asked them, his tone sharp.

'We don't know,' they replied. 'She went out about two hours ago and didn't come back.'

It dawned on him that what he had been dreading might have come to pass. He turned on his heel and ran as fast as he could to the barn where he had hidden the tailfin. When he got there he searched frantically but wasn't it gone.

Drunk and all as he was, he hurried down to the shore, hoping that his wife would be in her favourite place below the Bens, looking out to sea. She wasn't there. He ran like a man possessed to the Black Rock, but she wasn't there either. Not knowing what to do, he walked on along the shore, calling her name and cursing himself for his thoughtlessness.

Sunk in the depths of despair, he stood near the rock where he had first met her and cried out, 'Come back to me!'

Almost at once, he saw her rise out of the water and float close to shore. She held out her hand and he followed her into the waters of Tremone Bay.

Down through the years, many people have said that they have seen and heard Archie and Mara, their voices echoing in the breeze as they called their children to come to them. It is not known what happened to the children, but every so often the playful sounds of children's voices rise from two small,

*Archie's Craw.*

ghostly figures walking in the shallow water along the shore.

(Told by John McLaughlin of Gleneely.)

## The Bridgend Poltergeist

'There was a poltergeist in a house above Bridgend, where two men called Willie and Jim lived. Now, the last man to die in their house was a great man for gardening. When he was alive he had the loveliest garden you'd ever see in that locality. He grew every sort of flower you could want and there were beautiful coloured plants blooming all the year round. But it must be said that his greatest pride was his hedge and when he was no longer able to manage it his daughter kept it well clipped. It was straight and smooth and greatly admired.

'When he died his daughter went off to Australia and the garden became a bit of a wilderness, but the strange thing was that the hedge still looked beautiful and that was the mystery. Night after night, the whole street could hear the clippers going right around the hedge.

'The local people suspected that the garden might be haunted because Willie and Jim never set foot in it. Now, not far away Willie's cart was sitting resting on its shafts, but neither Willie nor Jim was inclined to use it, for, truth be told, they were somewhat lazy. Well, one night, people had gathered to listen to the clipping of the shears when there was an almighty crash and the cart shafts broke. Not a being was near it and sure everybody ran when the cart began to move of its own volition. Word went round that the last man to die in the house was angry and the crowd scarpered.

'But curiosity brought them back and the crowd was up at the house again. They were all waiting for something to happen. Willie and Jim came outside too

The Bridgend poltergeist.

and though nobody could see anybody clipping that hedge, it was nonetheless being trimmed by a seemingly invisible hand.

'There were two men among the crowd called McCann and McCutcheon who were scutchers. A *scutcher* was a worker who received flax stems from the farmer and had to hold the stems and scrape them with a wooden scutching knife and a small iron scraper. That left only the long flax fibres that would eventually be woven into Irish linen. It was a dirty job and very hard on the hands so it is no wonder that the scutchers drank. It has to be said that scutchers got a reputation of being very ungodly people because they were always drunk.

'Now McCann and McCutcheon were show-offs, so they leant up against the gable of the house and McCutcheon shouted at the top of his voice, "I fear neither God nor man!" And at that there came a great big stone that smashed into his jaw. It didn't fly straight because too many people were in the way. The people saw where it was coming from and how it turned nearly at right angles to avoid them and reach its target. I can tell you now that neither man was too emphatic about either God or man after that.

'I can tell you too, whether he believed in God or the devil, he never blasphemed again for everybody saw how the stone curved and moved to hit him on the jaw. You see, a poltergeist will throw a stone at you and it will come halfway and then it can turn right angles. They do that so you know it's something unnatural. They could throw something at a picture in your house and it could turn around and hit you, sitting over there on the opposite side.

'Anyway this thing happened at Bridgend but the activity of the poltergeist just died away through time and not too many would remember it nowadays.'

(Taken from an interview with Bertie Bryce.)

## The Devil's Elbow

This is a story about a man who lived in the parish of Culdaff in the 1850s, just after the Great Famine. He went by the name of Anton and he was a weaver, but the weaving trade had collapsed in the wake of the Famine. No one had money to spend on things like new clothes or blankets and he was forced to go out and work as a casual day labourer. He tramped the countryside looking for work, going around to various houses and farms, labouring on a day-to-day basis. His own farm was only about two or three acres and not enough to keep his wife and his large family. Occasionally he got work for a few days, particularly around harvest time, and that would tide the family over for a while.

When the light began to fail at the end of each day, the tired men went home and then they rose again in the early hours to work the next day and the day after that. At the end of the harvest, after the men had been labouring for several days, the farmer would call the harvesters into the farmhouse. It was customary for the farmer's wife to put out a bit of a spread with plenty of food and probably some *poitín* as well, as a way of saying thank you. Anton was a bit of a storyteller, so evenings were stretched out and it was usually after midnight when the men headed home.

They would go in twos or threes as they were scared of the darkness, especially after a good storytelling session about ghosts, banshees, devils and fairies. At that time of the night, it was pitch black in the countryside. They depended on one or two houses to have lights shining in the windows to help give them a sense of direction. Each house they spotted would be the welcome source of light, but on one night it was after twelve o'clock and there was blackness all around.

The other men arrived at their houses and soon Anton was the only one left. People were in bed, so with no lights and no sense of direction he headed down through the village, a place called Screen, and then to another place called Glack, near Glencaw. He felt very conscious of the fact that he was alone and he began to hurry, hoping that he was keeping to the centre of the road.

Just then he heard a strange sound, as if some sort of a creature was struggling in a 'shough' – a swampy kind of place – but there was nothing like that in the middle of the road. This being began to plod along beside him and Anton could hear the sound on the road clearly. The creature seemed to be quite large and Anton moved faster to get away, but it kept pace with him. When he slowed down, it slowed down as well. It was obvious from the rattling sounds it made that this eerie creature was carrying a chain. Once it struck Anton behind the knees and then whipped him on his side. It was clear to the frightened man that he was in danger. He tried to outrun the creature but the thing ran beside him until he got to the Devil's Elbow.

This bend in the narrow road between Culdaff and Moville was known to be haunted place. When Anton got there, the sky grew strangely light and he recognised where he was. He rushed to the

*Devil's Elbow.*

bend, knowing that if he got beyond it he would be safe. At the slope known locally as *Cúil an Diabhal*, he was beginning to feel a sense of relief but it was short-lived for the dog-like creature appeared before him. A strange light shone all around it, casting tree shadows on the ground. To his horror, Anton was confronted with the spectre of a black dog with an ungodly snarl and sharp, bared teeth through which black foam dribbled.

Later he said it was bigger than a massive wolfhound, with brutish, glaring eyes as large as saucers, ferocious-looking teeth and a reddish-black tongue.

To say that he was absolutely terrified would be an understatement. He was sure that this was the moment that he would be pulled apart in the animal's giant jaws, but something made him pull his rosary beads from his pocket. He held the crucifix part in front of his face and started to pray and as he did so the creature moved away. Holding the cross farther out in front of him, he repeated '*Téigh ar ais go hifreann!*' (Go back to hell!)

As Anton continued waving the crucifix and repeating the invocation, the animal seemed to explode and an overwhelming odour of brimstone permeated the air. A trail of vapour flew skywards. Anton found himself alone and shaken. He had no doubt in his mind that he had survived an encounter with the devil and that it had been driven away by the cross and the prayer.

To this day that place is still known as the Devil's Elbow or *Cúil an Diabhal*.

(Taken from an interview with Sean Beattie.)

# The Fahan Hill Poltergeist

On the hill above Duffy's Garage on the road between Derry and Buncrana sometime not too long after the First World War, strange things began to happen in a two-storey farmhouse that stands alone. It is surrounded by fields and enclosed by a stone wall on Fahan Hill just beside McCarron's Lane. The heather-clad hills rise behind it and one would think that it is a very peaceful setting for any house. However, according to local stories, the house itself was far from peaceful for many years.

There was once a 'Big Night' when many locals gathered there and the *craic* was good. The woman of the house was sitting on the armchair and the night was going well when suddenly the chair began to rise off the ground with the woman on it. A man made a grab for it, but it kept rising. A few other men tried to hold onto their friend and found that they couldn't let go. The chair seemed to have a force of its own. It catapulted itself out through the door and landed right into the centre of the midden out front. Now, the midden was the place where all the leavings of the cow barn were thrown to rot as compost. The woman, chair and all, landed right in the middle of this mess and the stench was unbelievably awful.

Apparently it was nearly impossible for that woman to be kept in the house and for whatever reason, no matter what she tried to do, she was pushed outside. It was reported in many newspapers at the time and when people gathered at night to see the 'performance' they were seldom disappointed.

The house was reputed to be haunted by a poltergeist. Burning sods of turf jumped out of the fire, singeing and burning the

*The Fahan Hill poltergeist.*

floor covering. Even when the owners removed the covering and left only the original flagstones, the hot embers hissed and spat, leaving burn marks on the stones. Drawers flew open without warning, scattering knives, forks and spoons all over the place. Often they flew through the air and changed direction randomly, a peril to anyone unfortunate enough to be in the kitchen at the time.

At bedtime the activity became more frantic. Bedclothes were ripped off and thrown about, accompanied by loud screeches. On one occasion the bed itself was supposed to have been flung forcefully against the wall. The occupants spent the night sitting under the broken frame, too terrified to move.

An explanation that was whispered at the time was that someone had brought a strange book into the house. Some said it was a 'bad' book and others that it was a book concerning the 'Black Arts', but no one really knows. Either way, it was a 'dangerous' book to read and once, when the woman was engrossed in it, an evil spirit took possession and drove her screaming from the house.

This happened several times and these fits were followed by strange maniacal outbursts until a priest was called to exorcise the house and the poor woman. He drove the spirit from the house, down the hill and into Lough Swilly and everything returned to normal. The woman's health improved, but the priest was seldom well after that. The exorcism had taken its toll.

Thankfully no more manifestations occurred and peace now reigns on Fahan Hill.

## The Witch of Loch a Duainn

Loch a Duainn is a lake near Kilclooney, which is a townland near Ardara in south-west Donegal. The lake can be seen from the road, but the island on the lake is not visible until you row out to the bend. At the centre of this small, dark island, there is a fort that is a replica of Grianan of Aileach in Inishowen. It is the same size and height, but more oval in shape. Few people went near the island, although fishermen sometimes fished in the lake as it had the reputation for containing rainbow trout and salmon.

It is said that a witch lived on the island in the middle of Loch a Duainn, which was part of the land that belonged to the O'Baoill clan. It is also said that the O'Baoills never ventured near there because they had heard of and experienced the witch's powerful spells.

She had a cow called Donn and the only 'friend' she had was a spider. She never left the island because she knew that if she came in touch with the water surrounding it she would lose her magic. Her cow Donn supplied milk daily and that was the only sustenance she had. Donn fed on the small patches of green grass and moss that grew inside and outside the fort on this otherwise bleak and rocky island.

The water lapped the edges of the grassy area and in some places the fort almost reached the water's edge, leaving barely any room for the witch to walk around it. No matter, for she rarely did so unless the cow had wandered, so she contented herself with walking and living inside the shelter of the fort.

Each morning she rose before sunrise, milked the cow and went back into the darkness, which she preferred. Inside the fort, the fairies were very active, but the witch had no time for them and when they disturbed her sleep one night she took a willow rod to them in anger. They retaliated by putting the 'blink' on her cow, which meant that the cow's milk dried up. She was so enraged that she had been left with no food supply that she decided to rid herself of the fairies. She knew a spell that she could cast to deal with the fairies once and for all. The spell was in the form of a mantra: *Cum cang cung! Cum cang cung!* The words did not make any sense, but whatever it was she said, it was magical because the faires were spellbound and could no longer approach the fort or her cow.

She might have had a suspicion that the fairies could find a way to harm the cow so at night before she went to bed she put a spell on Donn that turned the cow to stone. Before dawn she revoked the spell, milked the cow and took her supply of milk into the fort again. No one knew what she did under the cover of darkness.

One evening, a lone fisherman rowed towards the edge of the lake in his coracle. He saw the cow grazing close to shore and, afraid that it would scare the fish away, he gave it a wallop with the oar. Unfortunately, at that moment the witch was approaching, croaking out the mantra, so both the cow and the poor fisherman were turned to stone and fell into the water. The witch rushed to save the cow but as soon as she touched the water her magical abilities disappeared

*The witch of Loch An Duainn.*

and although she screamed and pulled at the stone cow it sank to the bottom of the lake and she sank with it.

A giant owl appeared and watched the water with its large eyes. When darkness gathered over the lake, the owl began to hoot unceasingly. It is said that this owl may be the reincarnation of the witch.

Fishermen, looking for their vanished friend, dared to approach the island, but were frightened away by the strange sounds of a cow in distress and the unearthly screeches of agony that they heard. There are some reports that the mantra drifts across the lake after sunset and before sunrise and that the owl stands sentinel over all.

Few people approach the island, but those who accidently do so behold the strangest manifestation of a demented woman who calls out: *Cum cang cung! Cum cang cung!*

The lake was a favourite place of the playwright Brian Friel. He and his father often went out there to fish when he was a boy and he described it as 'a magical place'.

(From an interview with Sean Beattie.)

# 6

# RESTLESS SPIRITS

## A Mother's Return

There are many stories throughout Ireland and indeed across the world about the tragic deaths of mothers, particularly after the birth of a baby. Yet it is often thought that when a mother dies and leaves very young children she still looks after them from the next world.

In earlier times, there were many such deaths, mostly due to a lack of knowledge about the complications of birth and also the fact that there was little skilled medical attention for poorer women. An untrained 'midwife' would generally have assisted these women when the time came to give birth. In each townland there was usually a woman who was called upon to bring babies into the world and to wash the dead who departed this life.

There was a young woman from Ballyheeney by the name of Kate McLaughlin who married Seamus O'Gallagher. They began their married life in Gortlesk and after a happy first year of marriage she gave birth to a baby boy. Tragedy struck when Kate died a few days after the birth.

Once the funeral was over and friends and neighbours had departed, Seamus was faced with the difficult task of looking after his new son. Kate's mother had stayed for a few days but was anxious to return home.

'Would you stay and look after the baby, Mrs McLaughlin?' he asked. 'A child needs a woman's touch.'

To his dismay, she refused, telling him that it would bring back too many memories of the daughter she had lost and that her other children needed her. He pleaded with her but to no avail. She was adamant that she could not stay.

Over the next couple of weeks Seamus did his best but the baby wouldn't settle. He was restless and cried often during the night. Seamus tried to wean him onto cow's milk but after a few mouthfuls the crying started again. The young man was at his wit's end.

'Lord, Kate, what am I to do?' he cried to his dead wife. 'For God's sake, help me. If our baby won't feed, he will surely follow you.'

He continued to pray that he would find the best way to care for the baby as he walked the floor with him each night. His heart was heavy with grief at the loss of his wife and he vowed that he would die rather than let anything befall his infant son. Somehow he would find a way to care for him. He prayed to his wife to show him how.

In her own home, Eilish McLaughlin, the baby's grandmother, was sitting alone about two weeks later at around the hour of midnight, awaiting the return of some of her family. It was a warm night and the half-door was open to let in the night air. She knitted as she waited, but stopped when she heard a sound outside. Eilish rose, but before she had moved two steps her dead daughter appeared, holding onto the half-door.

'Katie! Is it really you? Oh daughter, won't you come in?'

Eilish was overjoyed to see her daughter and reached out to touch her, but Kate looked at her with a sad expression and replied, 'Since you will not take my child, you will have no place for me.' She then disappeared as suddenly as she had appeared.

Eilish was shocked but did not hesitate. She grabbed her shawl, flung it around her shoulders and hurried off in the dark along the lonely Gortlesk Road. When she arrived at her late daughter's home, she heard the sound of the baby crying. She looked through the small window and watched her son-in-law pace up and down with her grandson cradled in his arms.

She knocked on the door and when he opened it she quietly whispered, 'I've come for the child.' She reached out, took the baby in her arms and his cries faded to a whimper. In a few moments the baby was asleep.

*A mother's return.*

Eilish gave no explanation as she and Seamus walked back to Ballyheeney, carrying the child, but she reared him with all the mother's love she had until he was old enough to return to his own home at the age of 14.

It was only later, when Eilish was on her deathbed, that she confessed the reason for her change of heart to Seamus.

He smiled and said, 'Sure, when I asked Kate to help me, she told me that you would come. Why do you think I didn't come after you?'

## Fanny Wylie's Bridge

Just on the border of Derry and Donegal is the village of Ballyarnett and beyond that a small stone bridge about twelve-feet long straddles the stream. It is known as Fanny Wiley's bridge.

It is an eerie place to walk past, particularly as darkness falls, for the sound of heavy footsteps can often be heard crunching along the road. The stories of the hauntings go back a very long time – as far back as the seventeenth century, it would seem.

In the Inquisition taken at Derry in 1609, this land was entered as the 'Quarter of Ballyarnell' although in the tithe-books it was named 'Ballyarnett'. The territory was awarded to Sir John O'Doherty, Lord of Inishowen by Elizabeth I and it included the townlands of Ballymagroarty, Coshquin, Laharden and Elaghmore. When Sir John rebelled in 1599, this land and the rest of Inishowen was forfeited. Sir John's son Sir Cahir was re-granted the land until he too rebelled in 1608, then the land was given over to Lord Chichester.

It would appear that Chichester was a cruel and vindictive landlord who did not tolerate tenants falling behind in their rents and he was known to have evicted several of them. He neither listened to promises nor gave those poor people any hope. It did not matter to him if they starved or died. Once evicted, he no longer had any reason to remember them.

One tenant, a small, wiry man with a facial deformity, lived in an area known as Derryvane. He had reason to remember Chichester and his land agent, who had evicted him during a severe winter. This man swore that he would not rest until his house was restored to him.

When someone was evicted, none of the neighbours could give shelter to the person for they risked being evicted themselves for doing so. Those who lost their homes were reduced to looking for shelter where they could find it, but sheltered places were few and far between. For a week following this particular eviction a neighbouring family housed the tenant in a small outhouse, but when word of the approach of the agent's thugs spread, the evicted tenant insisted on leaving. The neighbour's wife hurriedly gave him a woollen blanket as he sped away to find somewhere to take refuge out of the cold. The only shelter he could find was under a simple wooden bridge that crossed the stream some few hundred yards away.

During the next week, the bitter northerly winds brought snow and few people moved from their own fireside, but the neighbour and his wife could not help worrying about their friend. When the wind howled at its loudest and the heavy snow became a blizzard, she packed some food and warm milk and her husband fought his way through the deep snow to the bridge. When he reached it he called out but only the wind screamed in reply.

The neighbour searched around but found no footprints leaving the area. Fearing that the tenant was hurt, he slithered down the steep bank to look under the bridge. What he saw horrified him. His friend was lying stiff and cold with the freezing water of the Ballyarnett stream flowing around and over him.

The neighbour and his wife gave the tenant a Christian burial in their own small holding, as a result of which the land agent made life very difficult for them. One evening when the agent was returning from his rent collection, the ghostly figure of the man he had evicted jumped out of nowhere onto the parapet of the bridge, screaming abuse and threats. The agent took to his heels and refused to pass that way again. From that time on, there was talk that the restless ghost often appeared near and on that bridge, accompanied by the wind howling through the branches of the ivy-choked trees.

When the stone bridge was being constructed in the early 1900s, there was a small thatched cottage nearby, the home of the Wylie family. Joseph, who was a farmer, and Fanny, his wife, had eight children – three boys and five girls. Fannie, named after her mother, was the youngest and, it must be said, the favourite child.

Mrs Wylie was delighted that a bridge was being built because the old wooden one was a danger to her children. Often she walked across the field to see how the new bridge was taking shape, but she was puzzled to find that there were different workers there each time she looked. When she asked the foreman the reason for this, he took off his hat, scratched his head and asked, 'Are you a God-fearing woman, Missus?'

'Of course I am,' she replied. 'I'm a Presbyterian!'

'Well then,' he said, 'do you believe in ghosts?'

'Indeed I don't.'

'Well, the men who were working here certainly did because they said they've been sorely hampered from doing their work by the quarest-looking ghost ever to be seen. What could I do when they refused to work here but send them on to another job. They were saying that this should be called the ghost bridge.'

'Indeed it won't,' she said indignantly. 'I would be more willing to give it my name than one which would scare my children.'

'That would cost you five shillings,' said the foreman, more as a joke than a bargain.

When she heard that, she marched home, took down her money box from the mantle above the hearth and counted out two half-crowns. Five-year-old Fannie looked on and her mother bent to kiss her.

'Now my love, we'll have a bridge named after both of us.'

With that, she hurried out and slapped the money into the foreman's hand. And that is how the bridge got its name.

Although Fanny is long gone and the cottage is mere rubble, the stories of the ghostly appearances on the bridge persisted. Few people walked alone on that stretch of the road between Derryvane and Derry for when someone passed across the bridge the figure of a small, evil-looking man jumped out of nowhere onto the parapet of the bridge. He was said to leap about, muttering and growling and gesticulating wildly in front of the unfortunate person before disappearing into the darkness as suddenly as he had appeared.

But that was not to be the end of the tale.

*Fanny Wylie's Bridge.*

Those who experienced the manifestation were adamant that an eerie silence settled upon the bridge in the wake of his appearance and then an unearthly laugh more like a screech filled the air around them. When one traveller looked around, the burning eyes on that same evil face stared at him. The figure was crouched on the bridge, ready to spring into the air. Another man reported that the ghost jumped higher than the nearby tree and vanished, leaving only the echo of the horrible laugh.

The last known appearance was around 1962. The road is brighter now as new housing developments have crept out from the city, but the bridge is still there, as are the trees. People have said that when walking along the road at night they have heard the sound of uneven and strange footsteps, crunching on the gravelly road and making the hairs on the back of their necks prickle, but when they looked around there was nothing to be seen.

Could this evil apparition have been the ghost of the man who was evicted and died at that spot? Is the seventeenth-century tenant still seeking vengeance?

## The Ghost of Innishinny Island

On some of the islands lying off the coast of Donegal one could be forgiven for believing that time is standing still. They evoke traditional Irish culture in a landscape that is both barren and captivating. But that is not all that they evoke for the footsteps of times past are still heard on the islands and spirits still linger, especially on the small island of Innishinny.

Innishinny is one of the smallest and most beautiful of the Donegal islands.

*Innishinny.*

It lies beside the islands of Gola and Inismaan. These islands formed a safe anchorage for ships seeking shelter on the storm–battered Atlantic coast.

One Christmastide during the late 1800s, a small sailing ship trying to escape the stormy waves of the north Atlantic put into 'Gola Roads' anchorage for safety. The captain also intended to stock up on provisions from the village of Bunbeg since their food supply had become depleted during the prolonged storm.

Innishinny was a place they had visited before and they were content to stay in the waters some way inside the bar mouth for a few hours in the hope that the storm would abate. They were not alone as several people from the mainland were temporarily resident on the Innishinny. But something very strange happened that cast a shadow over the island.

In a letter, Mr T. McFadden wrote down the ghostly experience of his father, who was one of the men:

The old bar mouth at its best was never very safe for navigation, and this evening it was in its element, as with every storm it presented one boiling, seething mass of foam. The inhabitants of the island saw the frail small boat from the ship maneuver securely inside the bar, but prophesied some dire calamity should the captain and the two sailors venture to return to the ship that night. But the captain and his companions, having secured sufficient provisions, decided (as far as I can remember the story), even in spite of the entreaties of those on shore, to return to the ship. The storm was increasing, and what with their scanty knowledge of the intricacies of the channel, and the darkness of the night, certain it was that the next morning their craft was found washed ashore on the island, and the body of the captain was discovered by the first man who made the round of the shore looking for logs of timber, or other useful articles washed ashore from wrecks. The bodies of the two sailors were never recovered, and word was sent immediately to the captain's wife in Derry, who came in a few days and gave directions for the disposal of her husband's corpse.

After this terrible drowning, the island became a lonelier place for those few people who came to graze their horses and cattle during a few weeks of each year. To assuage their loneliness, they gathered together at night in one house to chat around the fire. But their peace was soon disturbed for on one dark and dismal night they heard steps approaching the door. It surprised them to hear the sound footsteps would make on rough, hard ground since they knew that the approach to the house was fine, soft sand.

The footsteps came closer and the men looked at each other in the full knowledge that there was no one else on the island save themselves. Each man turned to face the door, wondering who or what might be outside.

When the door swung open slowly, their curiosity turned to terror. A tall, broad-shouldered man filled the doorway, surveying those inside without speaking.

It was the captain who had been buried several days before! He was wearing the same seaman's suit and 'cheese-cutter' cap in which they had buried him. A woman, seated beside Thomas McFadden's father, said, '*Ar dheas Dé go raibh a anam*' (May his soul be at God's right).

Mr McFadden's spoke in Irish naturally and he bade the figure come in. '*Tar isteach*,' he said.

As soon as he spoke the words, the figure of the captain retreated and disappeared from sight. To a man, they rushed out but although they searched every part of the island they saw no one. Those who witnessed the ghostly sequel to the drowning accident swore to the truth of the story and carried that truth with them until their dying days.

## The Ghost of Terryroan

Terryroan is a small townland within Carromena, just a few miles from Moville. Now, in the 1880s the town of Moville was a point of embarkation for emigrants sailing to the New World.

It was a busy enough little town, with all the comings and goings, but there were plenty of local events as well. Fair Day was always held on the last Thursday of the month and farmers from all around brought their cattle for the event. There was much buying and selling and bargains were sealed with a spit on the hand and a slap. This was an honoured way of doing business and that slap was as sacred as any signed contract.

The women weren't left out. They brought eggs and butter to sell. Knitters and weavers usually had a good market for their wares as there were many old bachelors in need of a bit of help with such things. Journeymen tailors did a brisk trade, measuring up and making coats and britches for the farmers. These would always be ready for collection on the next Fair Day.

With so much going on, and the whiskey and poitín flowing freely in the taverns, there were many altercations and differences were often settled behind the bars with the exchange of a few blows and a free glass of porter.

Unfortunately though, one young-ish man called Willie D. was beaten up and sadly he wasn't able to rise and walk away. Some neighbours who saw his predicament half-carried him home, thinking that a good night's sleep would be the curing of him, but it was not to be. In the 1880s, it was hard to get medical attention and poor Willie never recov-ered. He died within six weeks, due to the lack of treatment for his injuries and Kitty, the girl that he was engaged to, was heartbroken. All the hopes and dreams she'd had of a happy life with Willie were buried with him.

It took a long time for her to get over his death and she rarely left the house. A fair while later, in the month of November, her mother persuaded her to go to a ceilidh in Moville, telling her that it would do her good to get out and spend time with friends her own age.

That evening when she set off there was no light from the moon. It was over-cast and cloudy and she began to get a strange shivery feeling. She tightened her shawl and walked faster but she could have sworn that she heard Willie's voice calling her name softly. She put it down to simply being nervous walking the road in the dark, but she was none-theless very relieved when she reached the ceilidh house. Inside, people were talking and laughing. In the flicker-ing candlelight, warmed by the turf fire in the hearth, everything shifted back to normality. It was only at the end of the evening that she whispered to a few friends that she was frightened to walk home alone.

'Sure, we're going that way anyway and we'll all walk together for none of us likes walking alone. You never know what might happen.'

The girls linked arms and set off, singing out loud in a fit of bravado. They hadn't gone very far when a hand reached out and grabbed Kitty's and began to pull her down a wee brae.

'Now, I know that wee brae,' said John McLaughlin, who recounted the story, 'and it might well have been the side of Mount Everest, but the Lord or whoever made them hold on to Kitty for dear life and the four of them were pulled, slip-ping and sliding down it.'

'I'll release you,' said Willie's ghost, 'if you go to the chapel to get lines for us to marry. But under no circumstances put your hand into the holy water font. When you've done that, I'll make a time for us to meet again and you must prom-ise to come.'

Well, Kitty was afraid to refuse and as soon as she nodded her agreement the hand let go of hers. The girls ran home and such was their fear that their feet hardly seemed to touch the ground. Word of the event went round and when the appointed day came Kitty knew she had to keep her promise to go.

The whole of Terryroan was there at the brae the next night as moral support when she went to meet the ghost. To her shock and amazement, the same thing happened: he started to pull and pull at her, trying to grab the papers, but she wouldn't let go of them. Her friends were all hold-ing on to her, but such was the strength of his ghostly grasp that he started to drag them down into the brae. They were so frightened that they called out for help. Some men rushed forward and held on until eventually they were freed.

Kitty brought the papers back to the priest and he in turn spoke to Bishop O'Kane of the diocese. Now, the bishop came to Moville to bless that spot and that was the end of it.

The local people had their own opinion on it all. The consensus was that Willie had been a jealous man in life and he couldn't bear to see her enjoying herself and maybe meeting another man, hence the marriage papers. He wanted to bind her to him in death as he hadn't been able to in life. He probably wanted her to enter his world.

The girl left Terryroan on one of the ships sailing to America. The neighbours went to the Bens and at the edge of the cliffs they set a huge fire to say farewell. It was a calm night and when the ship was 12 or so miles out they heard the blowing of the ship's horn, acknowledging the fire that illuminated the cliffs. It is said that a deep, mournful cry echoed across the water until the ship disappeared over the horizon.

(This story was told by John McLaughlin of Carromena.)

## The One-Armed Ghost

When an Anglican minister was installed in a rectory in a south-east Donegal parish in January 1900, he and his family were delighted. His wife had never settled into the town life of their previous parish and this was the answer to all their prayers – or so they thought.

The last incumbent of the Donegal parish had apparently departed rather hurriedly due to ill health and had left many of his belongings behind. From the first night that they entered the house, they heard strange and inexplicable sounds. In the beginning, for their own peace of mind, they tried to ignore the noises but when the volume of the sounds escalated to heavy thumps and bumps they began to feel quite afraid. It was as if the furniture was being disturbed, but when they heard what sounded like an animal running up and down the stairs at all times of the day and night they could no longer explain things away logically.

One morning when the wife came into the kitchen to light a fire in the range, the fire irons rose and smashed against the wall. She fled upstairs, calling to her husband that there was a 'presence' in the rectory.

But that was not all. Sometimes the noises came from outside and it seemed that some sort of malevolent being was kicking tin buckets around the yard in a raging temper. They even heard the heavy tramping of 'a herd of cattle' galloping past the rectory windows, but when they looked out they could see nothing.

Occasionally the noises settled for a few of months, but then they would start again more ferociously than before. The family's pet dogs seemed to sense the presence before anyone else and would make a terrible din. It was easy to see that the animals were terrified of whatever it was and they would bark at something in the hall that the family could not see. The dogs never approached the presence but backed away from it, barking and trembling.

One night one of the daughters went down to the kitchen at about ten o'clock for some hot water. She stood at the sink pumping the water into a jug and within a matter of seconds she felt the room grow icy cold. The hair stood on the back of her neck but she tried to dismiss the cold, shivering sensation by reasoning that she was only wearing a nightdress but the uneasy feeling that someone or something was watching her persisted and when she turned around she gasped and dropped the jug of water in shock.

Right in front of her stood a tall man, obviously with only one arm for an empty sleeve dangled from the shoulder of his long black coat. In his one arm he was carrying a lamp. He did not appear to notice her for he made no eye contact and walked out of the pantry into the kitchen and right through the kitchen wall. She ran to her parent's room in fright and told them what she had seen. They rushed downstairs but all was deathly still.

On another evening the younger daughter saw the same man walk down from the loft and go into the harness room. She ran to her father and told him, whereupon he went out immediately to confront the man but again he could see nobody. Another evening fairly soon after that, as dusk fell, his wife heard a knock at the hall door. Thinking that it was a parishioner looking for her husband, she went to the door and opened it. Standing outside was the man that her daughters had described. She had a terrible shock when he looked at her and walked through the walls of the house. She was rendered speechless and lay in a fever for several days, terrified of being left alone even for a moment.

At last she understood the previous rector's sudden departure. When they heard, the neighbours told of several attempts over the years to exorcise the ghosts, all of which had proved unsuccessful. The rector applied himself to the task and, according to a letter dated 25 November 1913, no noises or sightings occurred after that.

The family were left in peace for the tenure of the minister and subsequent tenants were not bothered by the strange manifestations.

*The one-armed ghost.*

## The Restless Spirit of Rosguill

The country at night is dark and there would be little or no light to help anyone travelling on the roads, so they wouldn't be travelling at too fast a pace. But when people had to walk a fair number of miles they would often call into different houses on their way home.

On one particular night a long time ago, a fella called John had left a ceilidh house and was making his way home alone. He was content enough for he had walked the road many a time and knew the way in both daylight and darkness. He was a bit surprised to hear footsteps behind him and after a couple of minutes he realised that there was someone walking alongside him.

The moon came out from behind the clouds and when he turned to look he got the shock of his life for he knew the man.

'But I also knew that that person was dead and I knew I wasn't imagining things,' said John. 'So I walked a bit faster but the man kept pace, walking beside me and I can tell you that I was scared witless. But then he moved so close that he nearly pushed me onto the grass verge beyond which there was a ditch. I didn't know what to do.'

At that time everyone would have carried rosary beads in their pockets.

'Well,' said John, 'I put my hand into my pocket and grasped the rosary beads. I held them so tight that it almost seemed that they were glued to my hand. I kept praying that the ghost would go but he stayed with me step for step. Then I got to thinking that the old people believed that a ghost can't cross water and I headed for the wee bridge that crosses the burn at the school.'

For John that wasn't the end of it. For what seemed like a long time but was probably only a minute or two, he couldn't pass the ghost. Each time he stepped to the side the spirit seemed to be there before him. But then it disappeared as suddenly as it had appeared.

Now, that incident weighed heavily on John for he knew the man well when he was alive. What terrified him was the fact that this man had come back to haunt him after he had been dead for a few years.

'I couldn't sleep for nights, thinking about what happened and asking myself if I had done something to the poor man to make him come back. The best thing I could do was to go to the priest and see what light he might be able to shed on it.'

'Father,' said he, 'there must be something annoying that man otherwise why would he appear to me?'

Well, the priest listened to what he said and then he opened his breviary and said a few prayers. When he closed his breviary again he looked at John and said, 'If anything like that happens again, it's very important that you ask in what way you can help the restless spirit find peace.'

Now, a few nights after that, the man appeared to John again and, thinking of what the priest had said, John had the courage to ask him what was wrong. The man answered that he had worked in Scotland and when he decided to come home one Christmas one of the men he worked with gave him a ten-shilling note to bring to his family for he couldn't afford to come home himself.

'But,' said John, 'it transpired that he never did give the money over to the family for he'd stopped in a pub or two on the way home and spent it and that had been weighing on his mind and annoying him.'

He then asked John if he could sort it out by giving the ten shillings to the family. The man said that that would that make him happy and give him peace. John promised that he would and went out of his way to pay that visit. The widow was puzzled as to why Joe would give her the ten shillings, but he decided not to upset her by giving her the full story. He said only that it was something he himself had promised to do.

A short time after that, when John reached the place where he had first encountered the ghost at the exact same time of night, a very bright light flashed and danced all around him. On this occasion John wasn't in the least afraid as he took the light as a sign that the man could now rest in peace.

That is the story that is often told in the locality of Rosguill and there's no reason to disbelieve it.

(Told by Joe Cullen, Rosguill, Fanad.)

## The Spirit of Sharon Rectory

Why would a quaint old-world rectory be singled out as one of Donegal's most haunted houses?

The house in question is Sharon Rectory. It was built by Trinity College just over a mile from Newtowncunningham, on the road to Letterkenny, and was completed in 1775, after fifteen years of labour. It was the High Anglican Rectory of Ireland and the stones were cut from Drumbee Quarry. Horses and carts transported the stones to the site, which lies not far from the shores of Lough Swilly.

The beautiful and tranquil setting befits the rectory, which, it must be said, is the last place one would expect to find a ghost. Yet it is well known that there have been strange happenings in this dwelling for over 200 years. Things really do go bump in the night

*Sharon Rectory.*

and there have been many sightings of the restless spirit of a lady, believed to be the ghost of Mrs Waller, the wife of the rector.

Many people have wondered about the reason for the haunting. The answer would seem to lie in the fact that the rectory was the scene of a gruesome double murder in 1797.

Lisa Tully, who lives there with her husband Vincent and their two daughters, recalled that they began encountering the ghost from the very first moment they moved into Sharon and sightings became quite regular.

'We moved in here in August and at the beginning we didn't know what it was making noises at night when we were in the bedroom directly above. We heard the sound of chairs scraping across the tiled floor in the kitchen. The original black-and-red tiles cover the kitchen floor and at that time we did not know that Mrs Waller died there.'

She went on to say, 'You would try to ignore the sounds but you would hear a cupboard door opening and closing. Pictures would fall off the wall but not straight down to the surface below. Where a piece of furniture was underneath, it seemed that the picture came out past the unit and projected itself outwards to fall on the floor. I would ask myself how that could possibly happen. This could be followed by a lot of doors banging.

'Then around June, it was a summer's evening and we were upstairs and had the bedroom window open and my husband Vincent heard this knocking on the window. After he closed the window, something else started. We had a big trunk at the foot of the bed with locks on it. The locks started to move with lots of rattling and when Vincent looked up he could see the vision of Mrs Waller. She was standing at the bottom of the bed.

'He didn't say anything in case it would scare me because he was going away for a few days and I would be alone in the house with my daughter, who was only 8 at the time. After that, Vincent didn't say or do anything but we still heard the knocks and the bangs, but we tried not to pay attention. There were things like the bathroom door handle rattling when someone went in but we always tried to find a logical explanation. "It's just new locks" and things like that, he would say, but he was just trying to make us feel better.'

Lisa Tully arranged to hold a séance in the hope that the ghost would settle. She firmly believed that the spirit of Mrs Waller needed to 'pass over'. It was thus that the story came out. Further research verified what happened on that night.

In the 1780s and '90s, there was massive support for the United Irishmen. In 1797, as people became mutinous, the Marquis of Abercorn's Donegal agent reported to his lordship:

> The entirety of your Lordships Estates as well in Tyrone and Donegal has been in so disturbed rebellious state that I have been obliged to enforce the rents by means of parties of the military. The ruffians style themselves as United Irishmen and proclaim for their object a reform of parliament. They are composed of all religions.

It was against this background of rising tensions that a double murder occurred at Sharon Rectory. Matthew Hood, Lands Steward, wrote to the Marquis of Abercorn on 7 March 1798:

At the residence of Reverend Doctor Waller, Rector of Wray Parish, Mrs. Waller and a Mr. Hamilton from Fanad were shot dead in February 1798. The Reverend William Hamilton had been working against the United Irishmen, trying to nip the insurrection in the bud.

At that time the Revd William Hamilton was the rector of Clondevaddock in Fanad and he, like most other rectors of that time, was a magistrate as well. In his exertions to avoid a full-blown insurrection, he had incurred the wrath of the whole countryside. Others blamed his high-handedness in dealing with those who were in rent arrears for causing many tenants to revolt against these acts.

Suffice it to say that Hamilton was active in detecting and bringing to justice the rebels called the United Irishmen. They marked him as a target and relentlessly pursued him in order to kill him. When his life was threatened, he decided to seek militia help from Derry but it was also suspected that he had gone to give information to the authorities regarding the state of the country. It is said that some persons who had reason to dread the information that Dr Hamilton was supposed to have given, followed him. Apparently on that particular date, en route to Derry, he had also attended the hanging in Lifford of a man he had sentenced to death.

The night was ice cold and stormy by the time he reached the Fort Stewart ferry on which he had to cross a stretch of Lough Swilly to reach Fanad again. The boatman refused to cross on account, it was said, 'of the terrible weather that evening'. It is supposed, however, that Dr Hamilton's enemies had ordered the ferryman to refuse the request to row him across the lough.

As the wind was getting stronger and the rain heavier, Dr Hamilton decided to seek shelter at the nearby Sharon Rectory, the residence of his friend, the Revd Dr Waller, Rector of Raymochey and a fellow of Trinity College, Dublin. Here he was made welcome. He sat down to share the evening meal with Revd Waller, his wife Sara and three ladies who were staying with them, two of whom were the nieces of Dr Waller.

At no time did Hamilton tell Dr Waller that he was a marked man who was undoubtedly being pursued by the rebels. Unbeknownst to Hamilton, on that particular night, his enemies had followed him and as the group of friends conversed over a delightful meal they heard the pounding of horses' hooves.

An armed band surrounded the house and demanded that Dr Hamilton be handed over to them. The muzzle of a gun was thrust through a window of the room in which they were sitting. The men shouted, 'We want bloodthirsty Hamilton!'

When this demand was not complied with, they fired through the dining-room window. Sara Waller rushed to protect her husband, who was paralysed on his left side and wheelchair-bound. Dr Hamilton followed and crouched at her side behind the wheelchair, bewildered and confused as the attackers fired.

What ensued was sheer bedlam!

Mrs Waller was a gracious and much-loved lady in the area. In her effort to save her husband she was wounded. The first shot struck Sara on the ear but still she remained at her husband's side. More shots were fired. Mrs Waller was struck in the shoulder and dropped to the floor. She attempted to crawl into the kitchen, but was hit once again and terribly wounded.

A servant, Barney McCafferty, carried her to the kitchen but she was bleeding profusely. The attackers were reportedly enraged when they heard they had wounded Mrs Waller and that Hamilton, their real target, was unhurt.

In the confusion of the moment, Dr Hamilton rushed for the stairs to the basement to escape the shooting, but the manservant Barney and another servant, helped by Reverend Waller's two nieces, dragged him out. It was said that he held onto the bannister of the stairs in desperation, whereupon one servant pushed a poker into the fire and brought it to the staircase, where they burnt Hamilton's hands until he was compelled to release his hold.

The talk at that time in the district was that the servants in the house sympathised with the attacking party and that they, contrary to the wishes of the family, pushed Dr Hamilton out.

Another interpretation of the event is that the servants were outraged that this man had brought death to their beloved mistress and they had no compunction in seizing him and casting him outside to the waiting men.

What is in no doubt is the fact that he was brutally murdered as he lay there on the stone step for in the morning his bloodied corpse lay stiff and cold. Not content with shooting and bludgeoning him, the attackers must have had his own horse trample Hamilton because in the morning the horse's hooves had his flesh and splintered bone on them.

After the rebels left, Dr Waller sent two horsemen post-haste to get Dr Blair for his wife but it was too late. Mrs Waller died from a massive loss of blood as she lay on the cold tiled kitchen floor.

Another account holds that Dr Waller and his nieces were so terrified that they ordered their servants to do this deed and that the Misses Waller were put on trial for this offence at the Lifford Assizes, but were acquitted.

Presbyterians were not treated well by the Anglican Church, which was the Established Church at that time. Suspicion fell on the Revd Francis Dill, who was the minister of Ray Presbyterian church. He was accused of being involved in the attack on Sharon Rectory, arrested and about to be sentenced to death when a member of his congregation testified that the Revd Dill was in his house visiting a member of his family who was dying. The murder charges were dropped.

Neither the perpetrators of this attack nor the weapon that fired the shots were ever discovered but news of the killings at Sharon Rectory spread like wildfire across the country between Derry and Donegal and many believe that the incident helped trigger the United Irishmen Rebellion of 1798.

The Revd John Waller died at Sharon two years later, in 1799. Future residents reported the ghostly sightings of a woman dressed in blue. The ghost, taken to be that of the shot Sara Waller, has been frequently seen over many generations and is in no way malevolent.

According to Lisa, 'You could feel her and hear her – the shuffles of the steps and soft swish of her dress. If anyone came into the house that wasn't a good person she would warn me. If I sat beside that person I would begin to shiver and I'd have to step away. At times of illness she would be here as a benign presence. I would always know that she is here.'

The woman appeared in a blue dress that glowed. There was no definition about the hands, feet or face, but she had blond hair with spiralling ringlets similar to the style of the late 1700s. Her ghost was seen in all parts of the house and one night Lisa awoke to see the lady in blue sitting at the bottom of the bed.

'It was as if she was mystified by the surroundings and there was a quiet sadness about her presence,' she said.

Other things manifest themselves in the rectory. Doors open and close and door handles rattle in empty rooms. Sometimes electrical gadgets fail to operate for no reason. One part of the house is distinctly cold – what is now the games room.

'One night near Christmas I just happened to be going out that door and I heard what sounded like a very loud, sharp crack and I saw a light right from the hall up to the other room. Another time I was walking past the dining room and glanced in and there was this beautiful blue light in the corner as well.'

Lisa said that in no way did she feel disturbed by the ghostly light.

'One summer's night we were lying in bed and I could hear the lock on the trunk at the foot of the bed rattling. I thought, "Oh, no, no." I didn't want to look up but something makes you look and as soon as I did, I saw her sitting right at the bottom of my bed. I could see her hair – even the little ribbon on it – but I couldn't make out any features on her face. It was like a mirage. I could see the bows on her dress and on the sleeves and I could hear the shuffling around the room when she moved. I reached over and put the light on but she was gone. There was nothing.

I looked around and put the light off again. I was really scared. I moved in behind Vincent and then I saw her again, facing me over Vincent's shoulder.

'"She's there," I cried again.

'"Where?"

'"There, standing beside you."

'Vincent stretched out his hand and literally swiped through her but he couldn't see her. He couldn't see her at all at that time. This went on night after night after night and I was the only one who could see her. She was standing at the foot of the bed. At that time, we dreaded going to bed because we just knew that she would be there again. It was scary. We weren't sleeping and I was thinking, "Please please, let us sleep tonight because we are just drained."'

Lisa said that that was the first night that they had slept in the last ten, but at six o'clock there was such an almighty bang of a door. It was as if she was saying, 'Up now, you have your night's sleep. I'm back.' They just knew that she was very unsettled and they were frightened.

'I began to think that she was there to give me a message or a warning because prior to that Vincent was digging a pool at the bottom of the garden with the help of my brother. I began to have reservations about the safety of having a pond when there were children about and my brother out of the blue said, "I don't think you should put a pond in because it could be dangerous."

'My husband was determined, but one of the nights when Mrs Waller's spirit was coming in and out I had this dream that my daughter had fallen into the pond and I couldn't find her. I stood at the side calling her and my dog was barking. When she came out of the water she was in the form of a little baby, just as if she had gone back to her birth again, and I had her wrapped up in a pillowcase. That night, when I woke from my dream, the ghost of Mrs Waller was sitting on my bed, looking at me as if in sympathy because I had lost my daughter. I felt a family connection and I knew she was there to give us a warning. We filled in the pond after that. Spirits get energy from your fear and they will drain that energy from you to keep themselves here. Your fear fuels them.'

Lisa has no doubt that holding the séance was a very positive step.

'Before we had our séance there were sceptics around the table: one was a newspaper reporter, but what she experienced that night totally changed her. We were there from midnight, but it was about 4 o'clock in the morning when the spirit of Mrs Waller was "passed over". Her spirit is at peace but she is still here in the house. This is her home but she is certainly more at rest.

All those taking part in the séance felt the presence of the spirit and they asked that it leave the family in peace. At this, a blue light rose up through the room and calm descended on Sharon House. Thereafter no further appearances of the woman in blue occurred. Having said that, Lisa Tully says that from time to time she is aware that something is about and noises can still be heard occasionally.

'I really don't mind if she puts in the occasional appearance. After all, we are happy here and she knows we'll do nothing to disturb her. I think her restless presence before the séance all goes back to the way she was murdered. Her life was taken from her and she probably did not realise what was happening at the time because it happened so quickly.'

Sara Susanna Waller, the ghostly tenant of Sharon House, lies alongside her husband John in a peaceful little graveyard near the shores of Lough Swilly, not far from her former abode. The stone reads:

In memory of Sara Susanna Waller
She met with an undesigned and
undeserved death
on 2nd March 1797.
She lived innocent and died lamented.

# 7

# TIME-WARP HAUNTINGS

## The Barnesmore Gap Mystery

The wild and lonely Barnesmore Gap cuts through the Blue Stacks Mountains in south Donegal. Many people who have travelled between Donegal town and Ballybofey have had the frightening experience of encountering the 'presence' of someone or something as they've made the journey alone through this barren place during the hours of darkness.

Very late on the night of 15 December 1964, a priest was making his way home from a function in Killybegs. He was quite relaxed and glad to be in a nice warm car because it was a bitterly cold night in January. The sleety snow fell heavily and was trying to obscure the windscreen but his wipers were valiantly keeping it clear. Still, he was anxious to get to Ballybofey as the weather was expected to worsen.

The snow seemed to speed horizontally towards the car and the headlights showed him that there were no other vehicles that might guide him and keep him safely on the road. He began to feel very uneasy as the wind rose and buffeted his small Volkswagen Beetle but pulling in was not an option. He was aware that the road had steep sides in several places. He prayed that there would be at least one other car on the road. Never had he felt as alone and vulnerable as he did on that awful night. He turned on his radio for company.

His spirits rose when he saw a light in the distance, but it was only visible for a few seconds and once it disappeared he was alone again, with the snow almost blinding him. He turned the windscreen wipers to maximum and peered out through the half-moon spot they cleared until it once more became obscured by snow, which was falling ever faster.

He was concentrating so intensely that he didn't realise the music had stopped until an there was an announcement:

Major Glenn Miller, the well-known American band leader, is reported missing. He left England for Paris nine days ago. Major Glenn Miller came over from the States early this year to direct the band of the AES, which has often been heard playing in the Allied Expeditionary Forces programme of the BBC.

The announcement was followed by one of the band's famous orchestrations. He listened for a few moments, not really thinking about the announcement, but with a sudden shock he re-ran the words in his head. Had it said that Glenn Miller had left England *nine* days ago? Was this some sort of joke? Was this some sort of appreciation on an anniversary or something?

Static interfered just then and the Beatles song 'I Feel Fine' blasted out of the radio. He felt uneasy, not just about the weather. There was something not quite right about the radio. He decided to investigate it when he got home – if he got home, he corrected himself.

He saw the faint glow of light in the distance and prayed that it was Ballybofey, even though it seemed too close to be the town. Still, if he got there safely he could stay with his priest friend and set off to Derry in the morning.

Just ahead of him, he saw a movement and, thinking it was an animal, he gently applied the brake, fearful that he might skid. It wasn't an animal but a woman standing almost in the middle of the road, waving him down. She looked almost blue from the cold, with eyes huge and black in her white face.

The car skidded some way ahead of her but before he had time to reverse backwards and put down his window she'd slipped into the back seat. He asked if she had been standing long but she didn't answer. He felt the cold creeping in from the rear and asked if she wanted the heat turned up. There was still no answer. He looked in the mirror but didn't see her and assumed that she was hunched down in the seat. He decided to turn up the heat and concentrate on his driving.

'Are you okay?' he asked, but he received no answer.

Barnesmore Gap's hitch-hiker.

'Will you let me know when you need to be left off?' he asked and this time he heard a whispered, 'Yes.'

He glanced in his rear view mirror a few times but still did not see her. He was in the act of adjusting it when he heard her call, 'Stop here.'

'But this is in the middle of nowhere,' said the priest.

She said, 'Pray for me, Father. This is where I died!'

He turned quickly but the back seat was empty. He had neither seen nor heard the rear door opening.

Before the priest moved off, he took a bottle of holy water from his bag and braved the snow. He sprinkled the water on the road, said a prayer and looked around. The snow eased off for a moment and he watched a bluish-white light rise until it was gone from sight. When he entered the car, he realised that he had not felt the cold as he prayed.

Later he discovered that a young woman had died on that stretch of the road in the 1940s. He checked with a friend in the BBC only to learn that no transmission had been made on that evening in 1964 about the disappearance of the bandleader.

The extraordinary coincidence of the apparition of the strange woman and the announcement of Glenn Miller's death remained a mystery.

## Mamore Gap's Ghostly Travellers

In the mid-1800s, many parts of Donegal were isolated, lonely places – none more so than Mamore Gap on the Inishowen Peninsula. The Urris Hills separate Dunree and Leenan and the Gap of Mamore was thought to be the sole gateway through these hills. The steepness of the rocky terrain made it a tough climb for any traveller and an insurmountable challenge for the Revenue men. It is therefore easy to believe that Urris was once known a 'Poitín Republic'. It was an ideal place for distilling whiskey and poitín. In any case, it was believed that the people of Urris were a hardy bunch and not the type of people with whom the authorities would meddle.

The rocky path, as it was then, rose to 700 feet and the loose rocks and scree slopes towered over the lonely track. If any brave or foolhardy man or woman happened to make their way up there at night, they made sure to stop at the holy well where St Columbanus is believed to have vanquished the water dragon Giollamach. There, they would pray for their safety on the journey.

Many filled a bottle with the holy water from the well and sprinkled it as they walked along, praying that 'their feet would keep them on the right path and the holy water would protect them from harm'.

People rarely ventured there in darkness as it was said to be haunted, although some claim that the illegal poitín-makers spread stories of ghosts and hauntings to keep people away. Maybe there is a bit of truth in this claim, but the following story of a ghostly encounter is one that has been handed down.

A man called Dan was setting off from Leenan to go to a fair in Derry with the intention of buying something for his poitín still. He did not want to advertise his mission around the townland since there was some jealousy amongst the poitín men, so he set off very early, during the hours of darkness.

As was often the case at four o'clock in the morning, the mist hung low at the top of Mamore, obscuring the summits of Craogh Carragh and Raghtan Mór. It swept down to the path itself and it was an eerie enough place to be walking alone. As he entered the misty heights, he was beginning to regret not having taken his wife's advice that he should avoid Mamore. He was nearing the crest when he became aware of the tramp of footsteps on the shifting gravel behind him. He felt relieved because the presence of other people would be welcome, or so he thought. He knew that part of the path was narrow and treacherous and he stopped to allow the others to pass by.

If he was hoping for some companionship on the journey, he was disappointed for, one by one, seven men emerged out of the mist and passed him, going in the same direction. He greeted them, as was his way, but they ignored his greeting, none of them uttering as much as a word. Now, that was unusual for it is known that country people are friendly and hospitable, especially in Donegal. He was disappointed, but prepared to set on his way again. Shortly after the seven figures had passed, another man approached from behind and called out a greeting,

'Where are you off to for the day?' he asked.

'I'm going to the fair in Derry,' replied Dan.

'Aye, we're going that way ourselves,' said the stranger. He paused for a moment, then added, 'Did ye ever sail in yon lough?'

'A few times but I'm a landsman. I'd rather feel solid ground beneath me,' said the Leenan man. 'What about yourself?'

'I've sailed around the world's oceans for many a year until I came to Lough Swilly. Did you ever happen to hear of a ship that was wrecked on the Swilly Rocks?'

'I did,' answered Dan. 'Sure, many a ship has been wrecked there.'

*Mamore Gap.*

'Indeed they have, but the one that we were aboard was the *Golden Fleece*.'

Now, Dan was a bit sceptical for he knew that the ship mentioned had gone down in 1817, but the more he quizzed the man the more he believed him. By the time they'd descended Mamore and reached the gentler road of Drumacrois, the sky was beginning to lighten. As they reached the top of that road, he heard a cock crowing in the farm below.

'It's a fine sound to hear in the morning and time for a rest,' he said and stopped to take out his tobacco and pipe, meaning to offer a smoke to his companion, but when he looked around there was neither sight nor smell of the man he'd been conversing with. Nor was there any sign of the other seven who had been walking about 30 feet in front of him in a group. He called and shouted until he was hoarse, but the only answer he got was the echo of his own voice.

When he reached Buncrana a few hours later, he stopped to visit an old relative of his. He began to relate his experience and was very surprised that the old man accepted it without any dissension.

'The Swilly isn't called the Lake of Shadows for nothing. Sure, if you have ears to hear you'll hear what you heard this day and a lot more, for there's hundreds of wrecks lying beneath its waters.'

'But what do you make of it?' asked Willie.

'All I can say is that few expected to meet their deaths here, but that's the way it was and there are many restless souls. All you can do is remember them in your prayers. That's all they are looking for.'

The Leenan man stopped at the holy well on his way back home and left eight stones on the prayer cairn for the eight spirits he had met on the lonely Gap of Mamore.

## The Battle of Sally Mackey

This is the personal story of a man who had a ghostly experience near Lifford in the nineteenth century.

It was a cruel winter in the Crimea in 1854/1855. Troops were suffering greatly from cold and sickness, but in Ireland gentlemen like William Mackey could still follow their sporting lives.

William was out shooting wildfowl near Lifford, but as midnight approached and the moon had all but disappeared he felt the cold creeping into his bones.

'It was time to set off for home,' he said later, 'but my attention was drawn to the barking of a dog close by.'

He stopped and listened and a few seconds later he heard a musket shot. His own hunting dog crouched in terror. As the shots continued to fill the cold night air, William became quite frightened for he had seen no other person in the vicinity while he was hunting. Then something very strange happened. A huge flame rose from the darkness just a few hundred yards from where he stood.

'At first I thought that a house was on fire,' he said, 'but I knew the area and I knew that there was no house there, nor was there anything else that could cause flames such as those that I saw.'

The debris of burning thatch and timber sparks began to fall and hiss as they showered into the water around him. The musket shots still resounded and just when the furious blazes reached their height the firing ceased and 'the clear sound of a bugle floated out in the midnight air'. When the bugle stopped, William heard the thud of cavalry coming at a canter. It was so real that he could hear the jingle-jangle of their equipage as they approached. They came to a stop at the scene of the fire and to William it seemed to be an eternity before they departed at a slow trotting pace.

William took the long way home and in the morning, when he related what had happened the night before to his father, he was sure that it would be dismissed as a bad dream. But it wasn't. His father explained that William was not the only one to have had that eerie experience. His father went on to tell the following story:

Sometime towards the end of the seventeenth century a widow called Sally Mackey lived near a small settlement. She had three sons who were accused of high treason and the officer in command of the regiment A Company stationed at Lifford was ordered to deliver the warrant. The troops set off from Lifford at 11 p.m. but when they reached the Mackey's cottage they had to approach in single file along the narrow bridle path.

When Mackey's dog began to bark it alerted the family. The first shot was the one that silenced their collie dog forever. As soon as the soldiers came into view the widow Mackey opened fire. The sons kept reloading the muskets and Sally Mackey killed and wounded several of them. The cottage went on fire but the woman continued firing and when the shooting stopped and the door was broken down the officer saw that although the three sons had perished their mother was still alive but severely wounded and burned.

She lived for several years after the incident and regaled anyone who would listen with the story.

After her death, the attack on the cottage was re-enacted by the ghosts of those who died there. Even though the cottage is long gone, the spirits still re-enact their violent demise to the present day.

## The Ghost of Nion Ruadh

There are many stories about the ghost of Nion Ruadh around the area of Clonleigh, near Castlefinn in County Donegal. This area of Donegal borders the River Foyle and County Derry and, farther south, Tyrone.

It is not known exactly who she is. Some people say that she is a princess from the Bronze Age who was buried on Croaghan Hill. Others say that she was the daughter of a Milesian chieftain who lived on Croaghan Hill. She supposedly drowned crossing a ford on the Foyle when she was going to visit her lover Ith, who lived in Ith's Glen near Glenmornin at Moorlough in County Tyrone. Another legend holds that she is Carolina Wilson, who was forbidden to see her lover and who drowned herself near where the apparition is seen in a wet marshland.

She is seen at different locations and was known to have appeared on the Craighadoes Road, also near Lifford, which, strangely enough, is the 'haunt' of Stumpy. The Glebe is a small townland outside Lifford and it is said that Nion Ruadh is buried in the trees at the end of the lane there.

Whoever she is, her appearance is frightening at times. Those who have encountered her ghost say that she wears a shawl – obviously not the garb of a princess! She keeps her head down and her body, dressed all in white, glows eerily. Other stories describe her garb differently.

The following are some of the stories of appearances collected by Belinda Mahaffy, a native of Clonleigh parish and a member of the executive committee of the Donegal Historical Society.

In the mid-1950s, Hugh Ban McGettigan of Clonleigh was finishing a night's work, setting rabbit snares on the lower slopes of Croaghan Hill. As the stars began to fade in the sky, he slung his pack over his shoulder and set off home. Before he'd gone very far, he was passing a stone pillar when, to his surprise, he spied a 'wee woman' disappearing behind it. He stepped around the pillar to see where she had gone and there she was, standing absolutely still. It wasn't quite light so he struck a match to see her better and two blue eyes stared back at him. She held his gaze for a moment before simply vanishing.

He described the face as very wrinkled, with a long chin. He wasn't frightened, just intrigued, and he had no explanation to offer for her appearance.

Phonsie French of Cavan Hill, Clonleigh, also had a story to tell about seeing a little woman walking near the Cashel at Craigadoes at the foot of Binnion Hill. 'About thirty-five years ago, every morning I went down Stumpy's Brae and over the road on the way to work when I saw her. She was wearing a scarf over her head. She was walking and walking, her feet moving always in the same spot but never advancing any further.'

In the 1970s, Mr Roulston of Cavanacor recounted that when he was about 17 years old he was walking home from a dance on a moonlit night. Where Dr Armstrong's house now stands, there was a gate where you could look down the fields towards the River Foyle.

When I walked as far as the gate, I saw a figure standing there, looking over the gate. The figure wore a long, grey cloak with a hood. As I walked past the figure, it turned to look at me and I saw that

*The ghost of Nion Ruadh.*

it had no face! I started running very quickly. I did not stop until I reached home. I never saw that figure again.

Odhran McGettigan of Coolatee, Clonleigh, had a spectral experience when he was returning home from Rossgeir pub one night after attending a football club meeting.

As I walked home past the Glebe, I looked up towards the trees at the end of the lane which leads up to the little empty cottage that everyone says is haunted. There in the trees, I saw a little woman with a pointed chin. She was wearing a grey linen pinafore dress with dark or navy spots on it. It must have been 9.30 or so at night. Just now as I am telling the story, I realise it was dark as I walked along, yet I saw her clearly, as though it were daylight. This event happened some years ago. I saw the little woman with the pointed chin only once. I have never mentioned this to anyone else before now.

Jim French of Porthall, Clonleigh, spoke of his experience.

'In the 1930s, my father Tom and his brother, my uncle Barney, followed the banshee along the banks of the River Foyle from the Kiln Knowe to the big drain at Legahullion. The tide was in so they could not cross over the drain but she just floated over it.' They described her as 'a wee woman wearing a cape with a hood over her head.'

Roy Colhoun of Lifford, Clonleigh, said, 'I had an uncle who used to fish at the Green Braes, which lies on the Derry side of Lifford. One day when I was a boy, he ran screaming into our house and threw himself down on the couch in the kitchen. He was pure white. My father asked him what was wrong with him and he said that he had been fishing down at the Green Braes during the night. At dawn, he saw a grey-cloaked figure standing further up the riverbank.

He thought his friends were playing a trick on him so he decided to get the better of them. He sneaked up behind the figure in grey and laid his hand on its shoulder. The figure turned round and instead of seeing one of his friends, he saw the face of a 'wizened old woman with a pointed chin'.

He screamed and fell back on the ground. When he looked up, the figure had vanished. He got to his feet and ran, still screaming, up the Green Braes, through the diamond in Lifford and up the Coneyburrow Road to his brother's home, where he threw himself down on the couch in the kitchen.

Margaret Edmundson of Clonleigh, Lifford, told this story in September 1997:

About a fortnight ago, the nightwatchman walked towards the main door of Strabane Tech. It was a Friday night about midnight and it was a windy and wet night. The watchman was about to lock up the Tech for the night. As he began to close the large main doors, he looked outside and noticed an enormous black dog standing outside the front door. The dog was staring intently at him. He didn't know where it had come from. He was sure he had not seen it walking behind him when he had first walked into the building. He was suddenly scared. He quickly locked the front doors and looked through a windowpane. A little woman now stood where the dog had been. She was very small with a pointed chin. She wore a long skirt that covered her feet and she also wore a shawl over her shoulders. She turned and began to glide east across the courtyard. As the nightwatchman looked on, she gradually rose up in the air and sailed over the school buses parked in the yard near the old Famine graves. She travelled on out of sight in the direction of Moorlough.

In September 2005, Brenda Mahaffy interviewed Adeline Maxwell of Cumberland Lodge, Clonleigh, and this is the tale she heard.

'When Joe, our eldest boy, was aged 11, just over twenty years ago, he saw a young girl walk up through the yard. She was 16 or 17 years old and had long fair hair that fell to the waist in two plaits. She wore a long grey robe that covered her feet. There was something strange about her demeanour. He saw her on

*Nion Ruadh Anvil Rock.*

several occasions and always ran away shrieking when this happened.'

Two elderly ladies felt her presence several times on the bridge over the Swilly Burn and refused to go that way at night. On at least one occasion, she passed straight through a gate just opposite their house. If locals are to be believed, she was following an old footpath. She moved over to Mullinaveigh and then on to Dromore Hill, where the Tourish family now lives. From there, she followed a path to the Mass Hill and stopped at the Rock on Mass Hill farm.

The Rock at Mass Hill is a large, anvil-shaped rock, which is believed to have some pre-Christian significance. Nion Ruadh is often seen at sites of pre-Christian importance. During Penal times, the Rock was used for the celebration of the Mass.

There are numerous stories of a little woman haunting a house in the Gort in the 1930s. The owner was a bachelor and finally drove off on his motorbike early one morning. He refused to return and sold the farm and emigrated to New Zealand within a fortnight. In the adjacent townland of Braade, the owner of a farm, also a bachelor, still refused to use the upstairs rooms of his home because of the 'wee woman who haunts there'.

The previous stories about Nion Ruadh are quite similar to the descriptions of banshees in other parts of Ireland. She appears as an ancestral spirit, an old hag, a young woman, a grey-hooded figure, a hooded crow, a stoat, a hare and a weasel – animals all associated with witchcraft in Ireland.

## The Green Lady
## of Ballyshannon

On Main Street in Ballyshannon, just north of the bridge spanning the River Erne, there is a particularly distinctive building that was built in the 1700s. It is a severe, plain, brick structure, as befits a military barracks, but to the locals still refer to it occasionally as the home of the Green Lady, although it now houses shops.

Who exactly was the Green Lady, you might ask?

According to a story in a New Brunswick newspaper, she was the neglected and unloved wife of a tyrannical and brutal major. It is said that she pined away for lack of love and it was suspected that her husband had something to do with her murder. She was also the daughter of a General Folliard, who had apparently arranged her marriage to the major.

Her ghost has haunted the barracks since 1776. It is said that after she was murdered her spirit continued to search for a soulmate to accompany her in the afterlife. But no one knows for sure. All that is known is that she fell in love with a young man, Edward Finlay, a handsome private and an exemplary soldier.

Ballyshannon was a garrison town in the eighteenth century. The major's regiment was stationed there in 1776. For some reason her husband, the major, took a great dislike to the young man. Perhaps he was jealous of Edward's good looks and popularity because the major was certainly neither handsome nor admired. He was a diminutive and ordinary man. Truth be told, he was hated for his hard-heartedness and it was often said that he should never have been given the privilege of wearing a sword or the king's uniform.

Whatever the reason, he ordered Finlay to do excessive and torturous duties and he never failed to berate the young man. After several days of suffering the acute embarrassment of being pointed out in the ranks by the gloating major and listening to the mortifying sniping about his suitability to be in the army at all, he was sickened at heart.

One afternoon, when the prospect of future years of ongoing degradation at the hands of his commanding officer threw him into deep despair, he began to think that he could never change his life. All the hopes and dreams that he had had of being a credit to his family and his country seemed doomed.

Just when he was at his lowest ebb, a woman clad in a silky green dress appeared on the parade ground and stared contemptuously at the major. She walked quickly down the front ranks, stopped in front of Edward Finlay and in a distinctly compassionate voice addressed him.

'Edward Finlay, are you tired of your life in this regiment?'

Edward raised his head and answered, 'I am.'

'Would you wish to exchange the discipline of the army and the tyrannical authority of yonder officer for the soft fetters of a woman's love and the obligations of duty resulting from the same?'

'I would. Gladly!'

Then she whispered, 'Meet me at seven tomorrow evening in the abbey.'

She then presented him with a well-filled purse of gold and disappeared within a moment through the barrack gate.

The major and the rest of the officers who had heard the exchange were speechless. Never in the history of a regiment had anyone cast such a look of disgust at their commanding officer, though many had often wished to do so.

Private Finlay's comrades who had seen the lady in green questioned him, wondering how he had come to know such a beautiful woman. They were curious and envious, but he couldn't give them an answer except to say that they knew as much about the matter as he did. He repeated that he had no recollection of ever having seen the lady before. He looked at the purse of gold in his hand to convince himself that it hadn't been a dream.

The men stood around joking with Private Finlay, which further enraged the major. He ordered them to their quarters and immediately set about plotting how to separate the young soldier from his good fortune. He needed an accomplice to do so. Corporal Terry McPhelim fitted the role admirably. McPhelim had carried out some questionable orders for the major, which had earned him a promotion to the rank of corporal. The corporal was sent to watch Finlay's every move.

The following evening, as the moon struggled to cast her light between heavy dark clouds, McPhelim quietly tracked Finlay's steps towards the abbey where he was due to meet the lady in green.

She appeared dressed exactly as she had appeared at the parade and declared, 'You have been true to the time, Edward Finlay, and I have only one request to make of you, which is a very natural one considering our situation. It is that you approach not any nearer to me than you now stand during our present interview. Remember on your peril that you conform to this wish. Now, tell me what I can do to relieve you in your present circumstances.'

Finlay stepped back a pace.

'First, may I ask to whom it is I am indebted for the friendly act of yesterday and for the more than friendly words which have brought me here this evening?'

He learned then that she was the daughter of General Folliard, who owned a grand home nearby, though she hastened to say that she no longer lived there.

When Finlay thanked her for the generous gift of gold, the Green Lady stated that the gift was in return for his love.

'Are you willing to assume the responsibility attached to my favour, if conferred on you? Are you willing to forsake the world and to share alone with me the happiness of one sole attachment, unequal though it may be, now and in future?'

Finlay replied, 'To be redeemed from my present bondage is to me a great consideration; but coupled with the thought of possessing the only one who has ever seemed to take an interest in my welfare, I cannot for a moment hesitate. I am yours on your own terms.'

'Very well', said the lady. 'You may now withdraw. Tomorrow I will take action to get you out of the army.' With that promise, she disappeared into the night.

Suddenly the major rushed out of the darkness towards the soldier and handcuffed him, then, surrounded by several soldiers, he was marched to the dungeon beneath the guardhouse where he was confined. Terrified at the probable death that awaited him, Finlay wondered how the Green Lady could help him now. She might even suffer public scandal if her declaration of love were broadcast to the world.

He spent a miserable night confined in chains in the dungeon, not even knowing what charge would be levelled against him. He was concerned for the lady who had shown him kindness and respect. At nine o'clock the next morning he was brought to face a judge.

Corporal McPhelim and the major had concocted a story between them. McPhelim swore that he saw Finlay in the act of changing clothes with a local man and heard him making plans to desert the army. McPhelim pointed at Finlay and stated that he had caught him in the act of making his escape. The major said little, leaving it to his corporal to give false evidence.

Although the court took pity on Finlay, they couldn't argue against the convincing testimonies and since this was in the period leading up to the 1798 Rebellion by the United Irishmen, deserters were automatically sentenced to death.

Edward Finlay was led forth for immediate execution. The firing party was chosen from his own regiment and ordered to prepare for their painful duty. They had to watch as their fellow soldier, with whom they had served, was marched to the selected spot to the sound of a muffled drum and a mournful dirge. The whole regiment formed columns along three sides of the square and Finlay had to pass his coffin, just a few paces from a freshly dug grave.

Finlay knelt down and the minister asked him to repent before taking his final leave of this earth. His eyes were covered so his executioners could not see the face of the man they killed. As he waited for the shots to ring out he wondered about his Green Lady and then, in an explosion of pain, death claimed him.

At that moment, as if out of thin air, the Green Lady appeared and, cupping Finlay's hands in hers, she leaned over his still form, which was oozing blood. A scream of anguish followed the volley and the lady's sudden appearance. It came from her father, General Folliard. Before

he collapsed insensible on the ground he cried out, 'Merciful Heaven! My Daughter!'

His daughter had died only a month before.

The Green Lady clasped Finlay in her arms and flew across the river to where it fell over a precipice. They paused for a moment, as if suspended on the surface of the water, and then floated over the precipice and were lost forever in the whirlpool below.

There are conflicting endings to the story. The first is that General Folliard slowly recovered and lived for several years thereafter. The second is that the brutal major who had made the life of Finlay hell died of shock when he realised that the lady was indeed his dead wife. In this ending, his co-conspirator, McPhelim, is ousted from the regiment.

As for the Green Lady and Private Edward Findley, it has been reported that the fated lovers' spirits haunt the abbey and sometimes on a calm, moonlit night the Erne fishermen see the ghostly apparition of the soldier and his spectral bride floating on the surface of the Erne. It is said that she has lately changed her green dress for a white one.

Her search for her soulmate ended in the spring of 1776.

### The Grianan of Aileach Warriors

They say that there is a cave under Grianan of Aileach that only opens once every seven years and for the short time that it is open you can hear ghosts moving around and moaning within.

In the 1880s, a man named McLaughlin who lived over beyond Burt was out hunting rabbits near the ancient fort very early one morning. When his dog started

*Grianan of Aileach.*

to bark in a frenzied way, McLaughlin thought that he must have cornered a fox. But when he approached the point where he had last heard the dog, it was nowhere to be seen. He called it several times and finally he came upon it, cowering between some large rocks. He couldn't understand what made his dog shiver with fright and knelt down to quieten it.

That's when he noticed some strange markings on one of the rocks. Curiosity made him investigate further. He realised that there was some sort of opening and when he pulled back the grass growing there he saw that this was no simple space. It was a portal entrance to the mouth of a tunnel, previously hidden by the long grass and heather. Now, he knew the locality well and had never seen this cave mouth before, so naturally he was anxious to know where it led.

He had listened to old stories around the hearth of hidden treasures far below Grianan and thought that there might be a lost fortune to be found if he were to explore further. He wound some of the long grass into a crude torch, lit it with flint from his tinderbox and went down into the cave. He was surprised that the cave narrowed into a kind of passage that extended way back into the rock.

The place was obviously very old indeed and a voice in his head told him to turn and run, but he was a stubborn man, and curious besides, so he simply tightened his hold on his gun. Cautiously he moved forward, holding the torch high above his head in his left hand until he reached the end of the passageway. He squeezed through a narrow crevice, which opened up into a huge, vault-like cavern. If the cavern was old, McLaughlin reasoned, then it was possible that the old stories were true and there might indeed be treasure of some sort near at hand.

As greed drove him forward his breath became a white cloud in a sudden chill that made him shiver. In the torchlight, he became aware that the walls seemed to be hung with rusted, ancient weaponry emblazoned with symbols. The torch was burning low and as it flickered the shadows seemed more menacing. McLaughlin felt afraid for the first time. Maybe his imagination was working overtime or maybe he had been in the cave longer than he thought, but he was sure that he heard the rustling of something not quite human in the dark recesses of the cavern.

Abruptly he turned to leave, but as he did so his eyes landed on a large gold horn high above him on the blackened wall. It hung almost beyond his grasp, so he put down his hunting rifle to stretch up to take the horn down. As he did so, the hair on the back of his neck stood up. He felt eyes boring into him and he slowly lowered his arm and felt around for the trigger of his gun. He was prepared to shoot whatever animal might come at him.

Only when he had his finger on the trigger did he swing around and in the torchlight he saw what he had first assumed were lumps of rock but now saw to be several figures lying stretched out on the cave floor. Huge axes and swords and other weapons unknown to him lay beside them, as if they had been left down temporarily. McLaughlin gazed at the figures and saw the rise and fall of their breastplates and the horrible truth dawned on him that they were not dead, as he had first thought, but sleeping. There was no sign or stench of bodily decay. Not even questioning how this could be, because his attention was on other things, he turned back to the coveted horn. He stretched a little more and lifted it down from the wall.

Some compulsion made him raise the horn to his lips and blow and at that moment one of the sleepers stirred in his sleep.

'Is it time yet?' the sleeper groaned in a rusty and gruff tone.

McLaughlin froze and stood in petrified silence as the owner of the voice made to rise. The stories he had heard in his youth were true! With a shudder, he realised that he had unwittingly stumbled into the ghostly world of ancient warriors and roused one of them.

He frantically tried to think back to what the old *seanchaithe* (storytellers) had said should anyone inadvertently wake the ancient warriors – answer them and they will rest again. In a trembling voice, he whispered, 'No, it's not time yet. Go back to sleep!'

But the ancient warrior was not soothed. He raised himself up and looked at McLaughlin with his glittering eyes and demanded in a stronger voice, 'Then why have you disturbed our sleep?'

McLaughlin noticed that several of the other sleepers were beginning to stir and his fear turned to absolute terror as an ancient hand grasped a mighty sword. McLaughlin dropped the horn and ran back towards the entrance passageway. Behind him he heard the creaking and clanging of metal weapons as the enraged figures rose to follow him. They were no longer silent, but bellowing in horrible, rasping voices, 'Why have you disturbed our sleep?'

Just as he saw daylight shine through the entrance to the cave, he felt someone grab his hand. With a cry of sheer terror, he pulled away and his rifle clattered to the ground. He threw himself onto the heathery ground between the stones outside the cave and rolled as far away from the entrance as he could. A wild crashing sound reverberated through the ground and somehow he pulled himself up.

When he looked behind, nothing remained of the hole. Even the high rocks had disappeared and only purple heather and grass remained. Too shaken to even walk away, McLaughlin sat and rested his head on his knees. Only when he felt his dog licking his hands did he open his eyes. Below him the waters of Lough Swilly glinted in the morning sun. He looked upwards. The proud, dark walls of the ancient fort of Grianan of Aileach dominated the skyline.

He wondered if the experience had all been a dream or perhaps a step back into the realm of imagination. As he searched for his hunting rifle, he passed the spot where the tunnel entrance had been and his dog growled, then his fur stood on end and he began to whine. McLaughlin felt the ground move beneath his feet and took to his heels, followed by his dog. He never did find his gun, nor did he ever hunt on the slopes of Grianan again.

Every seventh year the portal opens. If anyone is foolish enough to enter, they may never return. They will join the ghosts of the past.

## The Mysterious Woman in Blue

Buncrana was a small but vibrant seaside resort in the early thirties. People poured into the area, especially during the Scotch Fortnight when emigrants, mostly those who had gone to work in Scotland, returned to visit their families. The beaches were crowded on sunny days and parents kept a close eye on their children.

Once, the youngest daughter of a large Buncrana family went missing and her family went to the beach searching for her, but she wasn't there. They became increasingly worried when they found that no one could recall seeing her. As they turned to leave the beach, a young boy ran to them and said that he had seen a little girl playing near the river.

Greatly alarmed, they hurried to the Crana River, which flowed into Lough Swilly at the far end of the beach. They feared the worst because they were very aware that in the early 1920s, a young girl, Bridie, had been drowned in the river.

The little girl's sister Margaret, who had been left to look after the child, was in a dreadful state, afraid that her little sister too had drowned. She reached the bank of the pathway that led to the river and her heart lifted in relief when she saw a local man coming up the brae holding the child's hand. The child's feet and dress were wet but she was otherwise unhurt and as soon as she saw Margaret she ran to her.

The man explained how when he had approached the river wall, he saw a woman leading the little girl from the water. The woman was a stranger to him and, strangely, she was wearing a long blue dress. She spoke quietly to the child and although she called to him she did not come any closer. She simply asked him to return the child to her family.

'She seemed agitated,' he said, 'and she pleaded with me to tell this wee girl's mother that she must never go near the water alone.'

He assured the woman in blue that he would do so.

*The mysterious woman in blue.*

'Promise me,' she said, 'for the future is uncertain.'

Again he assured her that he would pass on the message.

When he had reached the road, he looked back, but the woman was nowhere to be seen. Leaving Margaret to relay the message to her mother, he went back to look for the woman, but it was as if she had vanished. The riverside was deserted.

Margaret hurried home, extremely relieved and thankful that her little sister was safe and sound. From then on, the little girl was not allowed to venture to the water alone.

Several years later, the little girl, now an adult and a sister in a religious order, was working in Naples. She held a very responsible position as a nursing tutor in a teaching hospital. One morning, in the company of another nun from Derry, she decided to go for a swim in the bay. Although she was a strong swimmer, a freak wave caught her and pulled her out to sea. At the same time, it threw her friend up on to the beach. Some men dived in and managed to reach the nun, but she was limp and unresponsive. When they brought her ashore, she was already dead. Such freak accidents were extremely rare on that beach and there was much grieving when her family in Buncrana heard the news.

The family still wonder whether her childhood experience and the Blue Lady's words of warning were predictions of the future. Who exactly was that woman who had rescued her from drowning when she was young?

# 8

# HUMOROUS TALES

## The Gaddyduff Miracle

It is always good to find a dash of humour when researching ghostly goings-on.

Just outside Clonmany, on the road to Urris and Mamore Gap, there are the roofless ruins of a little church founded by St Columb in the sixth century. Indeed, it was mentioned in connection with a rich monastery in the *Annals of the Four Masters*, but the incident that caused amusement locally took place in the nineteenth century when the little church, now Protestant, was undergoing repairs.

*Gaddyduff church.*

In the neighbouring village, there was a bandit known as '*Gaddydubh*' or the Black Thief. He had an accomplice in his shady trade and one night they planned to steal a sheep, break into the church, light a fire, boil some cabbage heads and have a feast. The thief sent his friend on his way to steal the sheep while he prepared the fire with some kindling. When the fire was lit, he put a large pot on to heat the water. While it was heating up, he placed the cabbage heads on a plank, ready to chop.

Now, there happened to be a rather short Scottish man called Ranald, of the Roman Catholic persuasion, who frequently visited his friend, a Protestant. On his way, he had to pass by the church and was surprised to see a light flickering there at that time of the night. He crept up to the door and peered through the keyhole and was horrified at what he saw – or what he thought he saw.

A tall, dark form wielded a cleaver and chop-chop-chopped at what the wee Scotsman thought were human heads. Beside him, a large fire burned below a cauldron that was spewing out clouds of steam. The chopped heads were being thrown into the steaming cauldron. The man ran to his friend's house as fast as his little legs could carry him but his friend was not in. His friend's mother sat there alone, a plump little woman who was crippled with rheumatism and unable to move without crutches.

Ranald burst into the room, breathing heavily and extremely agitated. He looked around wildly, then gasped out the shocking thing he had witnessed in the church.

'Jeannie, I see'd the divil in your kirk. He had a muckle pot and was boilin' awa' at bodies' heeds!'

'I widna believe that, Ranald. The divil couldna come into our kirk at all but if I could walk I'd go there to convince ye that yer mistaken.'

'Ne'er say it again. I'll carry ye,' said Ranald.

With that promise, he lifted the woman onto his back and set out for the church, staggering somewhat under her weight. When they arrived, there the black thief was, still alone. Upon hearing Ranald's footsteps, he thought it was his accomplice returning with the sheep. The thief ran to the window and said in a loud whisper, 'Is she fat?'

The old woman gasped. Terrified, Ranald dropped her onto the gravel path and ran like the hammers of hell back to her house. What happened next could be considered a miracle. Jeannie fearing that she was going to be the next meal for the devil, scrambled to her feet, jumped over the graveyard wall and reached her house before Ranald.

Strange as it may seem, that woman never felt a pang of rheumatism from that night until the day she died.

When the black thief died, the townland retained the name of Gaddyduff in memory of the strange cure of the crippled woman.

# BIBLIOGRAPHY

Allingham, H., *Ballyshannon: Its History and Antiquities* (Londonderry: James Montgomery, 1879).

Bell, D. & Flanders, S., *The Londonderry and Lough Swilly Railway: A Visitors Guide Co Donegal Railway*, Vol. 2 (Donegal Town: Restoration Society, no date).

Bonner, B., *Our Inishowen Heritage* (Limerick: Salesian Press Trust, 1984).

Bratton, R., *Round the Turf Fire* (Dublin: Talbot Press, 1931).

Byrne, P.F., *Tales of the Banshee* (Cork: Mercier, 1987).

Campbell, P., *The Ghosts of Inishfree & Other Stories* (Amazon CreateSpace, 2015).

Coghlan, R., *A Dictionary of Irish Myth and Legend* (Wicklow: Donard Publishing Company, 1979).

Cooper Foster, J., *Ulster Folklore* (Belfast: H.R. Carter Publications 1951).

Corcorran, J.A., *Irish Ghosts* (Geddes & Grosset, Scotland 2001).

Curran, B., *Beasts, Banshees, Beasts and Brides from the Sea* (Belfast: Appletree Press, 1996).

Curran, B., *A Bewitched Land* (Dublin: O'Brien Press, 2008).

Danaher, K., *Folktales of the Irish Countryside* (Cork: Mercier Press, 1967).

Doherty, J. & L., *That Land Beyond: Folklore of Donegal* (Derry: Guildhall Press, 1993).

Donegal Historical Society, *Donegal Annual/Journal of the County Donegal Historical Society* (2005).

Dunne, J.J., *Haunted Ireland* (Belfast: Appletree Press, 1977).

Fox, A.W., *Haunts of the Eagle* (London: Methuen & Co., 1924).

Frazer, J.G., *The Golden Bough* (London: McMillan & Co., 1894).

Gregory, Lady Augusta, *Complete Irish Mythology* (London: Octopus Publishing Group, 1994).

Hurrel, J., & Lewis, R.L., *A History of the Unexplained (Source Book)* (London: Flame Tree Publishing, 2003).

J.A.H., *Dublin Penny Journal*, Vol. 4, No. 186 (1836).

Joyce, P.W., *Old Celtic Romances* (London: Wordsworth Editions, 2000).

Lysaght, P., *The Banshee* (Dublin: O'Brien Press, 1986).

McCormack, K., *Ken McCormack's Derry* (Dublin: Londubh Books, 2010).

Maghtochair, *Inishowen: Its History, Traditions and Antiquities* (Mrs Peggy Simpson, 1867).

*New Brunswick Reporter & Fredericton Advertiser*, Vol. III (Fredericton, 1847).

O'Farrell, P., *Superstitions of the Irish Country People* (Cork: Mercier Press, 1978).

Rowan, A., *North West Ulster* (Middlesex: Penguin Books, 1979).

Scott, M., *Irish Ghosts and Hauntings* (Warner Books, 1994).

Royal Society of Antiquaries, *The Journal of the Royal Society of Antiquaries of Ireland*, Vol. 9 (1890).

Royal Society of Antiquaries, *The Journal of the Royal Society of Antiquaries of Ireland*, Vol. 9 (2013).

Seymour, St. John, & Nelligan, H., *True Irish Ghost Stories* (Dublin: Allen Figgis, 1969).

Smith, D., A *Guide to Irish Mythology* (Sallins, Kildare: Irish Academic Press, 1988).

Twiss, R., *A Tour in Ireland in 1775* (London, 1776).

Wilde, W.R., *Irish Popular Superstitions* (Shannon: Irish University Press, 1852).

Wilson, I., *Donegal Shipwrecks* (Coleraine: Impact Printing, 1998).

Winn, C., *I Never Knew that about Ireland* (London: Macmillan, 2007).

Yeats, W.B., *The Celtic Twilight* (Dorset: Prism Press, 1990).

## Websites

Finn's Valley Online, www.finnvalley.ie/places

Paranormal Database, www.paranormaldatabase.com/ireland/donegal.php

'Irish News', *Independent* website, www.independent.ie/irish-news

Dúchas, www.duchas.ie

## Interviewees

Sean Beattie, Donegal Historical Society
Bertie Bryce, Inch, County Donegal (RIP)
Seamus Gallagher, Dunlewey, County Donegal
Michael McGuinness, Derry (RIP)
Alistair McLaren, Stirling, Scotland
John McLaughlin, Carrowmena, County Donegal
Other people who wished to remain anonymous

## Excerpts from

Belinda Mahaffy, Donegal Historical Society
Ian Cullen, *Derry Journal*

## Newspapers

*Derry Journal*
*Donegal Democrat*
*Dublin Penny Journal*
*Londonderry Sentinel*